CHANGE AND CONTINUITY

Statute, Equity, and Federalism

CHANGE AND CONTINUITY
Statute, Equity, and Federalism

W. M. C. Gummow

OXFORD
UNIVERSITY PRESS

OXFORD

UNIVERSITY PRESS

Great Clarendon Street, Oxford ox2 6DP

Oxford University Press is a department of the University of Oxford.
It furthers the University's objective of excellence in research, scholarship,
and education by publishing worldwide in

Oxford New York

Athens Auckland Bangkok Bogotá Buenos Aires Calcutta
Cape Town Chennai Dar es Salaam Delhi Florence Hong Kong Istanbul
Karachi Kuala Lumpur Madrid Melbourne Mexico City Mumbai
Nairobi Paris São Paulo Singapore Taipei Tokyo Toronto Warsaw

and associated companies in Berlin Ibadan

Oxford is a registered trade mark of Oxford University Press
in the UK and in certain other countries

Published in the United States
by Oxford University Press Inc., New York

British Library Cataloguing in Publication Data

Data available

Library of Congress Cataloging in Publication Data

Data available

ISBN 0–19–829823–4

1 3 5 7 9 10 8 6 4 2

Typeset in Palatino
by Cambrian Typesetters, Frimley, Surrey
Printed in Great Britain
on acid-free paper by
Bookcraft Ltd., Midsomer Norton, Somerset

Contents

Table of Cases

Introduction

In what follows I am concerned with themes of continuity and change, particularly as manifested in Australia, but also with reference to other common law jurisdictions. These themes appear in the course of considering the relationship between statute and the case law which interprets it, the interaction between equity and statute and, finally, the operation of that form of legalism known as federalism.

I begin my consideration of the manifestation of continuity and change in these fields by asking what are the requirements of legal scholarship in an ultimate court of appeal in the common law world? Sir Robert Menzies once pointed to one of them. He did so when addressing the High Court of Australia on the occasion of the retirement in 1964 of his one-time pupil-master, Sir Owen Dixon. Menzies emphasized the need to see 'through the textbooks and statutes to the historic background and thus [determine] the significance of every change'.[1] The Prime Minister stated that, in his judgments, Dixon had 'woven the stuff of legal history into the fabric of modern statute and modern decision'.[2] That characteristic helps explain why those judgments have lasted and continue to exercise what often is a decisive influence upon Dixon's successors.[3]

The process to which Menzies referred is a striking characteristic of the common law system and one which underpins and renews its claim to popular acceptance. The general is developed from the particular and the law itself provides a bridge across which society moves from the past

---

[1] 'The Retirement of Sir Owen Dixon' (1964) 38 *Australian Law Journal* 3 at 3.
[2] Ibid., at 4.
[3] Four recent examples are *Ha v New South Wales* (1997) 189 CLR 465; *Lange v Australian Broadcasting Corporation* (1997) 189 CLR 520; *The Commonwealth v Mewett* (1997) 191 CLR 471; *Garcia v National Australia Bank Ltd* (1998) 72 ALJR 1243; 155 ALR 614.

to the future. By this means, stability is encouraged and the cataclysmic avoided.

One of the most perceptive of Australian observers (who, not by accident, is a poet) recently identified one consequence. It is that, while stability may be dull, a system that produces fewer graves than in lands with a more 'interesting' twentieth-century history allows breathing space to the people. Since the establishment of parliamentary systems in the 1850s in what were then the Australian colonies, political authority has passed without bloodshed from one administration to the next. Questions and conflicts of the greatest magnitude have been debated by reference to the legalities involved and resolved in the courts or at the ballot box. 'We owe this', as Malouf puts it, 'to the dullness of our British origins.'[4]

Of course, in Australia, it was apparent from the outset that there could be no continuity in development from those origins without adjustment and therefore change. The Imperial Parliament recognized this when enacting in 1828[5] that all laws then in force in England were to be applied in the administration of justice in New South Wales and in what later became Tasmania 'so far as the same can be applied within the said colonies'. In addition, the conditions of life in the colonies called for legislation on a scale and of a nature which was not then seen in Britain. After the establishment of self-government in the colonies, grants of Crown land were by or pursuant to local statute. A myriad of tenures with no precise common law counterparts was provided by statute and may be identified under the generic heading 'pastoral lease'. The system of title by registration, identified with Torrens, made conveyancing a process quite different from that in England. The Torrens system has spread far beyond Australia[6].

---

[4] Malouf, *A Spirit of Play: The making of Australian consciousness* (1998) at 28.

[5] Section 24 of 9 Geo IV c 83, known as the *New South Wales Constitution Act*.

[6] See, for example, *British American Cattle Co v Caribe Farm Industries Ltd (in receivership)* [1998] 1 WLR 1529 (Belize); *Gardener v Lewis* [1998] 1 WLR 1535 (Jamaica); Butt, 'Torrens around the World' (1999) 73 *Australian Law Journal* 18.

These statutory regimes inevitably leave spaces to be filled by equitable doctrines and remedies. Had equity not done so, and had the capacity of equity for adaptation been overwhelmed by statute, Australian property law would have been very different. The accommodation between these statutory regimes respecting land and the common law recognition of customary rights and interests enjoyed as an aspect of community life by the indigenous inhabitants remains a matter of controversy. All of the above displays in Australia particular tensions between continuity and change.

Further, the development of the basic structures and capital works for the conduct of trade and commerce, and the settlement of a growing immigrant population, involved the use on a significant scale of State controlled enterprises established by statute. It is no accident that those politicians who framed the Constitution in the 1890s were so concerned with provisions respecting railways, which were largely owned by the colonial governments.[7] The public service which administered the colonies, after control over it was wholly assumed from the Imperial authorities, was not left to the prerogative. It was put on a statutory basis. The result was to lay the ground in Australia for the development of what now is known as administrative law. It is no surprise that the framers of the Constitution made entrenched provision for the jurisdiction of the High Court to issue prohibition and mandamus and to grant injunctions against 'officers' of the new Commonwealth, nor that this term was readily taken to include Ministers of State for the Commonwealth. This was almost a century before the House of Lords decided *M v The Home Office*.[8]

Finally, processes of law were used to create the Commonwealth itself, its institutions and its written federal Constitution. It is worth recalling that, shortly after the United States had almost foundered in a war between the federal government and the secessionist states, and after

---

[7] This is reflected in the text of ss 51(xxxii), (xxxiii), (xxxiv), 98, 102, 104.

[8] [1994] 1 AC 377.

Bismarck had achieved German national unity by force of arms, not by the speeches and party resolutions of the Frankfurt Assembly of 1848 which he so despised, processes began in the Australian colonies which employed just those means to achieve, with popular participation, the establishment of 'one indissoluble Federal Common-wealth'[9] under the British Crown and under the Constitution.

The adaptation of British institutions to the federalism devised for the United States by those common law lawyers who assembled at Philadelphia in 1787 has brought with it, in Australia as in Canada, a new province for the rule of law and a distinct role for the courts. To determine a dispute between governments is to act on a higher plane to that engaged when quelling a controversy between citizens or between a citizen and the state. The construction of a statute, as a step in the application of that statute, is a different exercise from the determination whether a law itself can have no application, whether because it is beyond the competence of the enacting legislature or, if otherwise valid, is inconsistent with the law of another legislature in the federal structure. Inevitably, if not always consciously, in a final court of general appeal which also is a constitutional court statutory construction comes to be seen through a modified lens.

Contrary to the common law method to which I referred, to begin with a constitutional text against which legislative or executive action is measured is to proceed from the general to the particular. In that process, larger questions arise concerning the nature of law and of government under law. They cannot readily be avoided by a single-minded adherence to tenets of legal positivism and of parliamentary sovereignty and supremacy.

[9] The phrase used in the preamble to the *Commonwealth of Australia Constitution Act* 1900 (Imp).

[10] For their assistance in the preparation of the lectures for delivery and this text for publication I am indebted to my staff, Helen Holmes, Joshua Thompson and Russell Slatter, and my past Associates, Justin Hewitt and Andrew Gotting.

Lecture One—
The Common Law and Statute

The interaction between statute and case law is a matter of some complexity and gives rise to diverse issues. Those considered in this lecture include time and statute, the analogical use of statute in the development of the common law, the doctrine of the equity of the statute, the search for legislative intention, interpretation by the executive branch of government, and the action for breach of statutory duty, particularly duties imposed by a written constitution.

'OIL AND WATER'?

I begin with a point made by Professor Beatson. He has identified the dominant view (at least in the recent past) of the relationship between common law and legislation as one of 'oil and water'.[1] This observation was made before the statement by Lord Steyn in *Pierson* that '[u]ltimately, common law and statute law coalesce in one legal system'.[2] I would cavil only at the qualification 'ultimately'.

The one system spoken of by Lord Steyn must be syncretic. For example, laws such as the Statute of Frauds, the Statute of Limitations and the *Wills Act* have had a long life in many jurisdictions in the common law world. They have attracted considerable disputation and thus much judicial elucidation. The 'common law' represented by these decisions and the statutory text must be conflated to identify the normative structure which binds the community. That

---

[1] 'Has the Common Law a Future?' (1997) 56 *Cambridge Law Journal* 291 at 308.

[2] *R v Secretary of State for the Home Department, Ex parte Pierson* [1998] AC 539 at 589.

structure is not fixed, but changes to accommodate not only legislative amendment but also the outcome of further litigation.

Further, subjects which are thought of (and taught as) archetypes of common law doctrine may be so modified by statute as to have assumed a new character. Hence the statement:

> 'The law of torts comprises both common law and statute. It is not informed by any unifying principle or single underlying policy. It is made more complex by indirect interaction between common law and statute, through the action for breach of statutory duty and the potential development of analogical use of statutes.[3]

That is not all. In his influential paper 'Statutes and the Sources of Law',[4] Professor J M Landis emphasized that 'much of what is ordinarily regarded as "common law" finds its source in legislative enactment'. This statement was adopted by Harlan J in delivering the judgment of the United States Supreme Court in *Moragne v States Marine Lines, Inc*,[5] to which reference is made later in this lecture. Landis went on to refer to the 'definite statutory origin' of conspiracy[6] and continued:

> One needs only to recall such legislation as the Statute of Frauds or the Statute of Limitations to conjure up a vast body of law springing from parliamentary enactment and yet independent of its terms, even interpretatively applied.[7]

The whole of the doctrine of part performance, and the analogical operation in equity of the Statute of Limitations[8], illustrate the point. Landis concluded:

[3] The Hon Justice R S French, 'Statutory Modelling of Torts' in Mullany (ed), *Torts in the Nineties*, (1997), ch 7 at 211.

[4] Pound (ed), *Harvard Legal Essays* (1934) 213 at 214.

[5] 398 US 375 at 392 (1970).

[6] See *Peters v The Queen* (1998) 72 ALJR 517 at 526; 151 ALR 51 at 64.

[7] Pound (ed), *Harvard Legal Essays* (1934) 213 at 214.

[8] *Knox v Gye* (1872) LR 5 HL 656 at 674; *Cohen v Cohen* (1929) 42 CLR 91 at 99–101; *Motor Terms Co Pty Ltd v Liberty Insurance Ltd* (1967) 116 CLR 177 at 184–5.

> English and American land law responds to the
> same tests and reveals upon analysis that many
> of its germinating ideas have a statutory origin.[9]

The eyes of the most sober property lawyers gleam at the recall of the admonition by the then editor of the *Law Quarterly Review*[10] that, despite Lord Diplock's observations in *United Scientific Holdings Ltd v Burnley Borough Council*,[11] the Statute of *Quia Emptores* was still a pillar of the law of real property.

In addition, in various English colonies, including those which became the United States of America, fundamental laws required the application therein of English law as it stood at a particular date.[12] The common law of England was construed to include laws such as *Quia Emptores* and the Statute of Uses because they had been so incorporated into the fabric of English law that the whole was unintelligible without them.[13]

However, the 'oil and water' view has, in some measure, obtained in Australia. Ninety years ago, Pound spoke of the orthodox treatment of legislative innovation as being to 'give to it a strict and narrow interpretation holding it down rigidly to those cases which it covers expressly'.[14] The history of workers' compensation legislation in Australia is an illustration. Following a restrictive interpretation given to such legislation by the Privy Council in 1949,[15] it was not until 1996 that the definition therein of the term 'injury' was finally determined, in *Zickar v MGH Plastic Industries Ltd*,[16] to apply where a worker collapsed at work after the rupture of a cerebral aneurism. The aneurism was a congenital weakness. The term 'personal injury arising ... in the

---

[9] Pound (ed), *Harvard Legal Essays* (1934) 213 at 214.
[10] P V Baker QC, 'The Future of Equity' (1977) 93 *Law Quarterly Review* 529.
[11] [1978] AC 904 at 924.
[12] See *Delohery v Permanent Trustee Co of NSW* (1904) 1 CLR 283 at 310–11.
[13] *Van Rensselaer v Hays* 19 NY 68; 75 American Decisions 278 at 280–2 (1859).
[14] Pound, 'Common Law and Legislation' (1908) 21 *Harvard Law Review* 383 at 385.
[15] *Slazengers (Australia) Pty Ltd v Ivy Phyllis Eileen Burnett* [1951] AC 13.
[16] (1996) 187 CLR 310.

course of employment' was defined to include the acceleration of any disease to which the employment was a contributing factor. On the other hand, the *Trade Practices Act* 1974 (Cth) on occasion has evoked responses which would have agitated Pound. *Webb Distributors (Aust) Pty Ltd v Victoria*[17] concerned the application of the new remedial provisions of that law to the rule in *Houldsworth v City of Glasgow Bank*.[18] Four members of the High Court[19] remarked that the Act was 'unquestionably a piece of innovative legislation' but held that 'it is not to be seen as eliminating, "by a side-wind",[20] the detailed provisions established for more than a hundred years to govern the winding up of a company'.[21]

Recent decisions of the United States Supreme Court upon the interpretation of federal statute law have been criticized by Professor Strauss[22] as taking 'an essentially static and oppositional view of the task of statutory interpretation'. Statutes were regarded by the Supreme Court as 'binding so far as they imposed a meaning, but not instructive, not illuminated either by their political history or by the course of their implementation' and not as an invitation to the 'judicial partnership' of which Pound[23] and Harlan Fiske Stone[24] had spoken. Professor Strauss concludes that:

> This approach reverses understandings that
> long predate the New Deal, about the need to

[17] (1993) 179 CLR 15.

[18] (1880) 5 App Cas 317; see now *Soden v British & Commonwealth Holdings plc* [1998] AC 298 at 326–7.

[19] Mason CJ, Deane, Dawson and Toohey JJ; on the other hand, McHugh J said (at 41) that he could see no justification for reading into the unambiguous words of the statute 'some implied limitation on their use in relation to companies in liquidation'.

[20] See *Parkdale Custom Built Furniture Pty Ltd v Puxu Pty Ltd* (1982) 149 CLR 191 at 224 per Brennan J.

[21] (1993) 179 CLR 15 at 37.

[22] Strauss, 'On Resegregating the Worlds of Statute and Common Law' (1994) *The Supreme Court Review* 429.

[23] Pound, 'Common Law and Legislation' (1908) 21 *Harvard Law Review* 383 at 385.

[24] Stone, 'The Common Law in the United States' (1936) 50 *Harvard Law Review* 4 at 12.

accommodate the growth of statutes and administration as sources of law. It resegregates the
worlds of statute and common law.[25]

It is not the objective of this lecture to venture any opinion whatever as to whether these criticisms are well
founded. Their present significance is that they forcefully
illustrate with current reference the continuing tensions
between the common law and statute.

To an extent the metaphor of 'oil and water' to which I
have referred is an expression of the attitudes with which
practitioners have become imbued in the course of their
legal education. For example, whilst with my contempo-
raries I studied the local representatives of the great nineteenth-century English codifications of the laws of bills of
exchange, partnership and sale of goods, we were left to
wrestle with topics such as illegality in contract and trusts.
We were given no real appreciation of what was involved in
that aspect of 'public policy' which responded to proscrip-
tion of conduct by statute. Again, in conflict of laws,
statutes of the forum which controlled what otherwise
would have been the proper law of a contract were
regarded with little favour.

In Australia, the course of judicial decision in the High
Court of Australia should, at least in time, bring about a
considerable modification in these attitudes. First, as to
conflict of laws, there has been a series of decisions in which
statutory regimes modified or rendered void what otherwise would be contractual rights and obligations and
which supplied their own criterion to limit any apparent
universality in their operation.[26] These decisions respond to

---

[25] Strauss, 'On Resegregating the Worlds of Statute and Common Law' (1994)
The Supreme Court Review 429 at 527–8. More recently, it has been said that the
Supreme Court 'has come to recognize the deficiencies of textualism': Solan,
'Learning Our Limits: The Decline of Textualism in Statutory Cases' [1997]
Wisconsin Law Review 235 at 239.

[26] *Kay's Leasing Corporation Pty Ltd v Fletcher* (1964) 116 CLR 124; *Meyer Heine
Pty Ltd v China Navigation Co Ltd* (1966) 115 CLR 10; *Freehold Land Investments Ltd
v Queensland Estates Pty Ltd* (1970) 123 CLR 418; *Goodwin v Jorgensen* (1973) 128
CLR 374; *Akai Pty Ltd v People's Insurance Co Ltd* (1996) 188 CLR 418.

a legislative pattern exemplified in Britain in the exchange control law dealt with in *Boissevain v Weil*.[27]

Further, in *Duncan v McDonald*[28], the New Zealand Court of Appeal has identified a 'sea change' which is occurring in the general law of illegality. The cases in question are those in which a contract or trust, whilst not directly contrary to the provisions of the statute by reason of any express or implied prohibition in that statute, is attacked under 'the policy of the law' by reason of association with or furtherance of illegal purposes.[29] The identification of such a policy will involve close consideration of the scope and purpose of the particular statute. Recent Australian decisions[30] suggest that in such cases the tide is flowing in the direction of a flexibility which will enable the courts in the administration of equitable or restitutionary remedies to qualify or displace, wholly or in part, what once would have been a blanket refusal to enforce legal or equitable rights by reason of 'illegality'.

TIME, STATUTE AND COMMON LAW

The statement by Francis Bennion that a statute 'takes on a life of its own' and 'resembles a vessel launched on some one-way voyage from the old world to the new'[31] has its admirers both in the United Kingdom[32] and the United States[33]. The relevant passage deserves repetition in full:

> Each generation lives under the law it inherits.
> Constant formal updating is not practicable, so
> an Act takes on a life of its own. What the origi-

---

[27] [1950] AC 327.   [28] [1997] 3 NZLR 669 at 684.

[29] Cf Atiyah, 'Common Law and Statute Law' (1985) 48 *Modern Law Review* 1 at 14–15.

[30] In particular, *Nelson v Nelson* (1995) 184 CLR 538 (a trusts case), to which might be added *Fitzgerald v F J Leonhardt Pty Ltd* (1997) 189 CLR 215 (a contracts case).

[31] Bennion, *Statutory Interpretation*, 3rd edn (1997) at 687.

[32] Beatson, 'Has the Common Law a Future' (1997) 56 *Cambridge Law Journal* 291 at 303.

[33] Eskridge, *Dynamic Statutory Interpretation* (1994) at 49.

nal framers intended sinks gradually into history. While their language may endure as law, its current subjects are likely to find that law more and more ill-fitting. The intention of the originators, collected from an Act's legislative history, necessarily becomes less relevant as time rolls by. Yet their words remain law. Viewed like this, the ongoing Act resembles a vessel launched on some one-way voyage from the old world to the new. The vessel is not going to return; nor are its passengers. Having only what they set out with, they cope as best they can. On arrival in the present, they deploy their native endowments under conditions originally unguessed at.

This description is particularly apt to illustrate the situation where statute takes a particular common law doctrine as a criterion for its operation. The scope and purpose of the statute will expand, contract and diversify to follow the shifts in the common law. In this way, the common law gives to the statute a dynamic operation which, if differently expressed, the statute might not have had.

A notable example is provided by the Sherman Act, enacted in 1890.[34] Section 1 thereof states:

> Every contract, combination in the form of trust or otherwise, or conspiracy, in restraint of trade or commerce among the several States, or with foreign nations, is declared to be illegal.

Shortly after the passage of the statute, in giving the judgment of the Court of Appeals for the Sixth Circuit in *United States v Addyston Pipe and Steel Co*, Circuit Judge Taft said that it was:

> certain that, if the contract of association which bound the defendants was void and unenforceable at the common law because in restraint in trade, it is within the inhibition of the statute if the trade it restrained was interstate. Contracts that were in unreasonable restraint of trade at

[34]   26 Stat 209.

8 *Lecture One*

common law were not unlawful in the sense of
being criminal, or giving rise to a civil action for
damages in favour of one prejudicially affected
thereby, but were simply void, and were not
enforced by the courts.[35]

After referring to various English authorities including
Mogul Steamship Company v McGregor, Gow & Co, his
Honour continued:

The effect of the act of 1890 is to render such
contracts unlawful in an affirmative or positive
sense, and punishable as a misdemeanor, and to
create a right of civil action for damages in favor
of those injured thereby, and a civil remedy by
injunction in favor of both private persons and
the public against the execution of such contracts
and the maintenance of such trade restraints.[36]

More recently, in *State Oil Co v Barkat U Khan*, O'Connor J,
when delivering in 1997 the opinion of the Supreme Court
of the United States, said that:[37]

the general presumption that legislative changes
should be left to Congress has less force with
respect to the Sherman Act in light of the
accepted view that Congress 'expected the courts
to give shape to the statute's broad mandate by
drawing on common-law tradition'.[38] As we
have explained, the term 'restraint of trade', as
used in §1, also 'invokes the common law itself,
and not merely the static content that the
common law has assigned to the term in 1890'.[39]

Similar considerations are involved with the development in patent law of the phrases 'inventor' and 'manner of

[35] 85 F 271 at 278–9 (1898); affd *Addyston Pipe and Steel Company v United States* 175 US 211 (1899).
[36] 85 F 271 at 279 (1898); affd *Addyston Pipe and Steel Company v United States* 175 US 211 (1899).
[37] 139 L Ed 2d 199 at 213 (1997).
[38] *National Society of Professional Engineers v United States* 435 US 679 at 688 (1978).
[39] *Business Electronics Corp v Sharp Electronics Corp* 485 US 717 at 732 (1988).

new manufacture' used in s 6 of the *Statute of Monopolies* of 1623. In *National Research Development Corporation v Commissioner of Patents*,[40] Dixon CJ, Kitto and Windeyer JJ said that what was involved was an inquiry into the scope of the permissible subject-matter of letters patent and grants of privilege protected by s 6. They continued:

> It is an inquiry not into the meaning of a word so much as into the breadth of the concept which the law has developed by its consideration of the text and purpose of the *Statute of Monopolies*.[41]

A related, though distinct, situation arises where equity, in formulating the law as to permissible charitable purposes, has relied upon the Preamble to the Elizabethan statute.[42] In the course of deciding that the provision of facilities for cremation qualified as a charitable purpose because there was sufficient analogy in cases dealing with burial to bring it within the statute, Lord Wilberforce said:

> The purposes in question, to be charitable, must be shown to be for the benefit of the public, or the community, in a sense or manner within the intendment of the preamble to the statute 43 Eliz I, c 4. The latter requirement does not mean quite what it says: for it is now accepted that what must be regarded is not the wording of the preamble itself, but the effect of decisions given by the courts as to its scope, decisions which have endeavoured to keep the law as to charities moving according as new social needs arise or old ones become obsolete or satisfied.[43]

The long administration of the patent law and of charitable trusts provided a source of vitality to old law.

The prospect of which Bennion spoke is made more immediate in cases where the substratum or necessary

---

[40] (1959) 102 CLR 252 at 269. See also *R v Patents Appeal Tribunal; Ex parte Swift & Co* [1962] 2 QB 647 at 657–8.   [41] (1959) 102 CLR 252 at 269.

[42] 43 Eliz I c 4.

[43] *Scottish Burial Reform and Cremation Society v Glasgow Corporation* [1968] AC 138 at 154.

assumptions upon which a particular common law doctrine has rested are removed by statute. Once '[t]he whole reason and justification'[44] for the common law doctrine or requirement has gone, the latter goes with it. There are difficulties in ascertaining whether rules of the common law disappear where, by reason of legislation, their reason no longer holds, and in the operation of the maxim *cessante ratione legis, cessat lex ipsa* expressing that notion.

These difficulties appeared in an acute form after the passage in the second half of the last century of legislation improving the status of married women. The House of Lords and the High Court differed as to whether, as a consequence of the provision in the *Married Women's Property Act* 1882 (UK)[45] and its Queensland counterpart that each married woman was to be capable of suing or being sued as a *feme sole*, the husband remained liable at common law with his wife for torts committed by her during joint coverture. The High Court held that the husband's liability was gone.[46] In *Edwards v Porter*,[47] by majority, the House of Lords later reached the opposite conclusion. The American courts tended to the same conclusion as the High Court and also generally absolved the husband of liability for antenuptial contracts and for torts of the wife.[48]

Professor Freund pointed out that in such cases the courts do not achieve the result by construction of the statute, but deal with the common law itself and with the relation between the rule of the common law and the reason for it. He continued:

> On the basis of the altered relation a court may go so far as to eliminate an existing special rule of law, but it can hardly create new obligations not previously existing. Thus it has not been

---

[44] *Edwards v Porter* [1925] AC 1 at 10.   [45] 45 Vict c 75.

[46] *Brown v Holloway* (1909) 10 CLR 89 at 98, 104, 107.

[47] [1925] AC 1 at 17–18, 35, 46.

[48] J M Landis, 'Statutes and the Sources of Law' in Pound (ed), *Harvard Legal Essays* (1934) 213 at 223, 238–41.

suggested that the new rights of a married woman impose upon her new duties of support, but correlative positive obligations of this kind can only be recognized if created by legislation.[49]

In *Thompson v Australian Capital Television Pty Ltd*,[50] statute[51] abolished the rule that a cause of action against joint tortfeasors was one and indivisible. The consequence was a further change in the common law, not made by the statute itself, so that the release of one joint tortfeasor no longer released the others. The further practical consequence was the decline of the conveyancing device whereby a covenant not to sue, rather than a release, was taken. It is significant, for what follows below, that here the common law rule collapsed, not by reason of analogical use of statute, but because statute had removed an essential prop upon which the common law rule rested.

At the other extreme is *Lamb v Cotogno*.[52] There, the appellant failed to persuade the High Court that a consequence of a compulsory system of insurance in New South Wales was to render exemplary damages unavailable in that State against a defendant who was insured against the liability in question.

ANALOGY

When deciding *Lamb v Cotogno* in 1987, the High Court discountenanced the general proposition, attributed to scholars including Pound[53] and Atiyah,[54] that from statute

---

[49] Freund, 'Interpretation of Statutes' (1917) 65 *University of Pennsylvania Law Review* 207 at 225. See also Williams, 'Statutes as Sources of Law Beyond Their Terms in Common-Law Cases' (1982) 50 *The George Washington Law Review* 554 at 583–4; Epstein, 'The Static Conception of the Common Law' (1980) 9 *The Journal of Legal Studies* 253 at 268–9.

[50] (1996) 186 CLR 574.

[51] *Law Reform (Miscellaneous Provisions) Act* 1955 (ACT), s 11(2).

[52] (1987) 164 CLR 1 at 10–11.

[53] 'Common Law and Legislation' (1908) 21 *Harvard Law Review* 383.

[54] 'Common Law and Statute Law' (1985) 48 *Modern Law Review* 1. Professor Atiyah's views were commended by Cooke P in *South Pacific Manufacturing Co Ltd v New Zealand Security Consultants & Investigations Ltd* [1992] 2 NZLR 282 at 298.

there may be derived 'some principle to be applied by way of analogy in fashioning the common law'.[55] The Court apparently did not favour what it described as an 'attenuated version of the same idea'[56] expressed by Lord Diplock in *Warnink v Townend & Sons (Hull)*.[57] His Lordship there spoke with reference to the development of the tort of passing off in the light of consumer protection legislation which nevertheless did not create any civil action for breach of statutory duty. He said:

> Nevertheless the increasing recognition by Parliament of the need for more rigorous standards of commercial honesty is a factor which should not be overlooked by a judge confronted by the choice whether or not to extend by analogy to circumstances in which it has not previously been applied a principle which has been applied in previous cases where the circumstances although different had some features in common with those of the case which he has to decide. Where over a period of years there can be discerned a steady trend in legislation which reflects the view of successive Parliaments as to what the public interest demands in a particular field of law, development of the common law in that part of the same field which has been left to it ought to proceed upon a parallel rather than a diverging course.[58]

Much earlier, Cardozo J, speaking of a legislative policy as 'itself a source of law', had gone on to identify it as 'a new generative impulse transmitted to the legal system'.[59]

Something like this reasoning appears in the recent English Court of Appeal decision in *Attorney-General v Blake*.[60] The issue (resolved in the affirmative) was whether the Attorney-General might, 'as guardian of the public interest', bring proceedings for an injunction to restrain the

---

[55] (1987) 164 CLR 1 at 11.   [56] Ibid.   [57] [1979] AC 731.
[58] [1979] AC 731 at 743.
[59] *Van Beeck v Sabine Towing Co* 300 US 342 at 351 (1937).
[60] [1998] Ch 439.

defendant from receiving or from authorizing any third party to receive on his behalf payment representing the proceeds of his crime. In the United Kingdom, as in Australia,[61] legislation empowers courts to order the confiscation of the proceeds of crime. In *Blake*, the Court of Appeal set out 'the principle enunciated' by Lord Diplock in the above passage in *Warnink* and continued:

> In the legislation providing for court orders to confiscate the proceeds of crime Parliament recognised the public interest in promoting a policy of preventing a person from retaining property obtained by him as a result of, or in connection with, the commission of a criminal offence. The fact that the statutory machinery cannot be applied in the circumstances of this case, where the defendant has not been and, in all probability, will never be put on trial for his offence, does not detract from force of the policy in the context of the Attorney General's right, as guardian of the public interest, to bring proceedings in the civil courts to enforce that policy.[62]

Lord Diplock's statement also received attention from the High Court in *Public Service Board of NSW v Osmond*.[63] The issue was whether in New South Wales bodies exercising discretionary powers should as a general rule give reasons for their decision in the absence of any statutory requirement such as those imposed by federal law[64] and the law of Victoria.[65] The High Court decided that the common law imposed no such general obligation. Gibbs CJ said:

> Lord Diplock did not intend to say that because there has been a trend of legislation in one jurisdiction, the courts of a different and independent jurisdiction should develop the common law of that jurisdiction on a parallel course. Such a proposition would be as impossible to sustain as

---

61 For example, *Proceeds of Crime Act* 1987 (Cth).
62 [1998] Ch 439 at 463.   63 (1986) 159 CLR 656.
64 *Administrative Decisions (Judicial Review) Act* 1977 (Cth), s 13.
65 *Administrative Law Act* 1978 (Vic), s 8.

> it would be to put into practice when different
> States had taken different legislative courses. The
> common law of New South Wales cannot be judi-
> cially modified to make it accord with the statute
> law of, say, Victoria.[66]

These remarks are directed not so much to analogical use as such as to the application of the statutes of one jurisdiction to the common law of another jurisdiction.

Certainly before *Lamb v Cotogno* the High Court had spoken in a somewhat different vein. Against a background of statute, particularly Pt V of the *Trade Practices Act* 1974 (Cth), which gave extensive private remedies to consumers and competitors, the Court had to decide whether there was a common law action for 'unfair competition' or 'unfair trading'. In the course of deciding there was not, Deane J said in *Moorgate Tobacco Co Ltd v Philip Morris Ltd [No 2]*:

> The rejection of a general action for 'unfair
> competition' involves no more than a recognition
> of the fact that the existence of such an action is
> inconsistent with the established limits of the
> traditional and statutory causes of action which
> are available to a trader in respect of damage
> caused or threatened by a competitor. Those
> limits, which define the boundary between the
> area of legal or equitable restraint and protection
> and the area of untrammelled competition,
> increasingly reflect what the responsible
> Parliament or Parliaments have determined to be
> the appropriate balance between competing
> claims and policies.[67]

More recently, the High Court decided that, if it was ever the common law that by marriage a wife gave irrevocable consent to sexual intercourse with her husband, it is no longer the law in Australia, as it is no longer the law in

---

[66] (1986) 159 CLR 656 at 669. See also *R v Home Secretary, Ex parte Doody* [1994] 1 AC 531 at 564; Craig, *Administrative Law*, 3rd edn (1994) at 310–16. See further the observations of Mason J in *State Government Insurance Commission v Trigwell* (1979) 142 CLR 617 at 636.   [67] (1984) 156 CLR 414 at 445.

England.[68] Mason CJ, Deane and Toohey JJ said of the notion of irrevocable consent:

> The notion is out of keeping also with recent changes in the criminal law of this country made by statute, which draw no distinction between a wife and other women in defining the offence of rape.[69]

Their Honours referred to legislation in five of the States.

Further, Lord Wilberforce had disposed of the 'fundamental breach' doctrine in a fashion not dissimilar to that unsuccessfully urged with respect to exemplary damages in *Lamb v Cotogno*. In *Photo Production v Securicor Ltd*,[70] his Lordship referred to the situations in which it had been productive of injustice to leave exception clauses to operate, and said that, since then, 'Parliament has taken a hand', not with commercial contracts generally but with respect to the consumer contracts covered by the *Unfair Contract Terms Act* 1977 (UK). In other cases, 'there is everything to be said, and this seems to have been Parliament's intention, for leaving the parties free to apportion the risks as they think fit and for respecting their decisions'.[71]

The differences of approach revealed in these decisions reflect the tensions identified by Professor Strauss and referred to earlier in this lecture. Plainly, there is more to be said in this area. In particular, the Anglo-Australian courts sooner or later will have to face the implications, doctrinal and constitutional, in the statement by Professor Strauss:

> Legislative influence and statutes are extended when statutory policy becomes the basis for analogical reasoning to decide cases that have not been provided for. The judicial function is also augmented if the world in which judges act to promote coherence includes statutory as well

[68] *R v R* [1992] 1 AC 599 at 612.
[69] *R v L* (1991) 174 CLR 379 at 390.
[70] [1980] AC 827 at 843. The doctrine of fundamental breach had never been accepted in Australia: *Darlington Futures Ltd v Delco Australia Pty Ltd* (1986) 161 CLR 500 at 509–10.   [71] [1980] AC 827 at 843.

as judge-made law. Thus, to include statutes
implies that judges may shape their readings
within the possibilities offered by the text, over
time, as changing general law and the social
circumstances to which it responds may
suggest.[72]

In 1908, Pound had put at the top of the list of his
suggested interpretive devices the treatment of statutes as
active principles from which courts could reason by analogy.[73] Freund, writing in 1917 to like effect, had appealed to
what he perceived as the European practice of analogical
construction of their civil codes.[74] This emphasis upon
'analogical interpretation' was a significant feature of the
Progressive movement of which these scholars were
members. In 1970, it was favoured by the United States
Supreme Court in the statement by Harlan J:

It has always been the duty of the common-law
court to perceive the impact of major legislative
innovations and to interweave the new legislative policies with the inherited body of common-
law principles—many of them deriving from
earlier legislative exertions.[75]

'Analogical interpretation' is an element in the ebb and
flow of decisions in Commonwealth jurisdictions which
allow or deny general law remedies in addition to or in the
absence of express provision in remedial statutes. The topic
of statute and new private rights is one to be reached later
in this lecture. In other respects, there has been a lapse in

---

[72] Strauss, 'On Resegregating the Worlds of Statute and Common Law' (1994)
The Supreme Court Review 429 at 437. See also Finn, 'Statutes and the Common
Law' (1992) 22 *University of Western Australia Law Review* 7 at 18–25.

[73] Pound, 'Common Law and Legislation' (1908) 21 *Harvard Law Review* 383 at
385.

[74] Freund, 'Interpretation of Statutes' (1917) 65 *University of Pennsylvania Law
Review* 207 at 229–30.

[75] *Moragne v States Marine Lines, Inc* 398 US 375 at 392 (1970). See also Blatt,
'The History of Statutory Interpretation: A Study in Form and Substance' (1985) 6
Cardozo Law Review 799 at 841–5; Williams, 'Statutes As Sources of Law Beyond
Their Terms in Common-Law Cases' (1982) 50 *The George Washington Law Review*
554 at 584–8.

the transmission of ideas across the Atlantic and the Pacific.

Only now are Anglo-Australian courts beginning to deal with the issues involved. One, not dealt with very satisfactorily in the United States,[76] is whether a common law rule which reflects a statutory analogue is to be changed as the statute law is modified from time to time. Thus, where a statute of limitations is applied by analogy, the analogy has followed changes in the statute.[77]

Another issue was raised by Professor Atiyah.[78] He asked whether the alleged 'analogy' operated by way of 'extension' of the statute in question or 'to fill in the blanks' in a common law rule. The distinction may be illustrated by the decision of the Full Court of the Federal Court of Australia (Olney, Kiefel and Finn JJ) in *Adelaide Steamship Co Ltd v Spalvins*.[79] The *Evidence Act* 1995 (Cth) applied to the adducing of evidence in federal courts as to communications in respect of which legal professional privilege was claimed. It adopted (advertently) a criterion ('dominant purpose') which differed from that ('sole purpose') which in Australia[80] applies at common law. The statute applied only to claims made in resistance to the adducing of evidence at trial. What was to happen when privilege was claimed during discovery or in answer to interrogatories or other ancillary processes? Were different results to follow depending upon the point at which the privilege claim was made? Was it significant that only one State, New South Wales, had adopted the federal statute?

The Full Court answered these questions in *Adelaide Steamship* by deciding that (i) the statute had created a new setting to which the common law of Australia must adapt; (ii) the principles applicable at trial provided the paradigm;

---

[76] Williams, 'Statutes As Sources of Law Beyond Their Terms in Common-Law Cases' (1982) 50 *The George Washington Law Review*, at 593.

[77] See *Klin Co v New York Rapid Transit Corporation* 3 NE (2d) 516 (1936).

[78] 'Common Law and Statute Law' (1985) 48 *Modern Law Review* 1 at 12–15.

[79] (1998) 152 ALR 418.

[80] Since *Grant v Downs* (1976) 135 CLR 674; cf *Waugh v British Railways Board* [1980] AC 521; *Roma v Morley* [1976] 1 NZLR 455; *Secretary of State for Trade and Industry v Baker* [1998] Ch 356.

and (iii) having been changed by the statute, the remainder of the common law should reflect the new paradigm.[81] More recently, an enlarged Full Court (Black CJ, Beaumont, Sundberg, Merkel, and Finkelstein JJ) has taken a contrary view. In *Esso Australia Resources Ltd v Commissioner of Taxation*,[82] whilst there was acceptance by four members of the Court of the use of statutes by analogy to develop the Australian common law, the federal structure with its multiple legislatures inhibited the operation of the doctrine. Why, it was said, should the Australian common law be modified in response to statute law which did not apply in all courts? On the other hand, in the leading United States decision, *Moragne v States Marine Lines, Inc*,[83] Harlan J had applied the analogy principle. His Honour emphasized that in every State the common law rule denying recovery for wrongful death had been abrogated by legislation, although none could be relied upon directly to confer a right of action in federal diversity jurisdiction upon the plaintiff in respect of the death of her husband, a long-shoreman, who was killed in waters within the State of Florida.

Next, there is what is identified as the 'extension' of the operation of statute by judicial reasoning. This probably is better considered as a response to the 'equity' of the statute in question.

THE EQUITY OF THE STATUTE

Much of the difficulty which the courts continually encounter with statutory interpretation reflects the unsettling need to accommodate what one might call a socially directed rule, expressed as an abstraction, to the infinite variety of human conduct revealed by the evidence in one case after another. Added to that is the attraction, derived from equity rather than the common law, of substance to form and of the essential over the inessential.

---

[81] (1998) 152 ALR 418 at 428.   [82] (1998) 159 ALR 664.
[83] 398 US 375 at 390 (1970).

The prevalence of these notions throughout the corpus of the law was emphasized by Dixon and Evatt JJ in *Attorney-General (NSW) v Perpetual Trustee Co (Ltd)*.[84] Their Honours' immediate concern was with charitable trusts, the *cy-près* doctrine and the requirement of general charitable intention. In the course of expounding that subject they said:

> The truth is that the time-honoured distinction between essential and accidental characteristics is at the root of the test provided by the modern law for ascertaining whether a trust for charitable purposes, found incapable of literal execution according to its tenor, is nevertheless to be administered *cy-près*. In other departments of the law, however, similar distinctions are in use. Analogies may be seen in the question whether a contractual provision is of the essence; whether a term is a condition or a warranty; in the question whether invalid provisions of a statutory enactment or other instrument are severable or form part of an indivisible whole; in the question whether a law is mandatory or directory, and perhaps in the question whether the substantial purpose of creating a special power of appointment was to ensure a benefit to the objects so that they take in default of its exercise by the donee.[85]

The substance or essence of the form in which statutory norms are expressed, if astutely perceived, might accommodate the legislative purpose to the equity of the particular facts of the case. From such ideas there was derived the doctrine of the 'equity of the statute'.[86] Since the Year Books,[87] the phrase has been used in various senses, some

---

[84] (1940) 63 CLR 209.   [85] Ibid., at 226–7.

[86] See *Cofield v Waterloo Case Co Ltd* (1924) 34 CLR 363 at 371–2; *Nelson v Nelson* (1995) 184 CLR 538 at 552–4; *Byrne v Australian Airlines Ltd* (1995) 185 CLR 410 at 458; *Wik Peoples v Queensland* (1996) 187 CLR 1 at 184; Kelly, 'The Osmond Case: Common Law and Statute Law' (1986) 60 *Australian Law Journal* 513 at 515–16; Fricke, 'The Juridical Nature of the Action upon the Statute' (1960) 76 *Law Quarterly Review* 240 at 254–5.

[87] Thorne, 'The Equity of a Statute and Heydon's Case', (1937) 31 *Illinois Law Review* 202 at 208–9.

of which overlap.[88] However, for present purposes, the phrase may be said to identify a doctrine that the common law courts render more effective the legislative will or, more broadly, 'guided by the dictates of conscience and natural justice, could modify the rigor of a statute or apply its rules to cases not provided for, to avert hardship or injustice'.[89]

As is apparent from this statement, the doctrine might operate to *limit* the scope of one statute as well as to *expand* that of another statute.[90] In its first operation, the doctrine survives, and flourishes, though not under that name. It is invoked when courts emphasize the need for legislation to employ unmistakable and unambiguous language to interfere with important principles of government and of the rule of law.[91] So also when the courts declare that the propriety of departing from a literal interpretation 'extends to any situation in which for good reason the operation of the statute on a literal reading does not conform to the legislative intent as ascertained from the provisions of the statute, including the policy which may be ascertained from those provisions'.[92]

The development of the doctrine in England has been attributed merely to the extreme conciseness of ancient statutes and to the lack of precision in drafting which prevailed in past times.[93] This is to ignore the different perception in those times of the task of the judges and

[88] de Sloovère, 'The Equity and Reason of a Statute' (1936) 21 *Cornell Law Quarterly* 591 at 591–5; Plucknett and Barton, 'Introduction to *St German's Doctor and Student*' (1974) 91 *Selden Society* at xlvii.

[89] Loyd, 'The Equity of a Statute' (1910) 58 *University of Pennsylvania Law Review* 76 at 82. See also Thorne, 'The Equity of a Statute and Heydon's Case' (1936) 31 *Illinois Law Review* 202; Marcin, 'Epieikeia: Equitable Lawmaking in the Construction of Statutes' (1978) 10 *Connecticut Law Review* 377 at 392–7.

[90] Dickerson, *The Interpretation and Application of Statutes*, (1975) at 213–14.

[91] *Coco v The Queen* (1994) 179 CLR 427 at 435–8; *Commissioner of Stamps (SA) v Telegraph Investment Co Pty Ltd* (1995) 184 CLR 453 at 467–8; *R v Lord Chancellor, Ex parte Witham* [1998] QB 575 at 581.

[92] *Cooper Brookes (Wollongong) Pty Ltd v Federal Commissioner of Taxation* (1981) 147 CLR 297 at 321.

[93] *Wilson v Knubley* (1806) 7 East 128 at 136 [103 ER 49 at 52]; *Gwynne v Burnell and Merceron* (1840) 6 Bing (NC) 453 at 561 [133 ER 175 at 217]; *Hay v Lord Provost, &c of Perth* (1863) 4 Macq HL(Sc) 535 at 544.

assumes a refined conception of the separation of powers long before Locke took up his pen.

The search for the equity of legislation 'has become indispensible for civil code readers'.[94] For those members of the European Union with common law systems, this comparison may come to be a significant matter in their respective municipal systems. In the United States, though without any precise consensus as to its meaning, recourse still is made to the equity of the statute by opponents of non-literal construction.[95] Judge Calabresi appealed to it as a means of limiting the operation of what he saw as obsolescent (or obsolete) statutes.[96] However, so far in England, the doctrine in its expansive operation generally has been taken not to have survived the prevalence of Benthamite ideas and the rise of positivism.[97]

The influence of the doctrine is still to be seen in 'the policy of the law' which informs those cases upon illegality in trust and contract to which I referred earlier in this lecture. So also in the law of charitable trusts, to which I have already referred. This influence is reflected in the statement by Barwick CJ[98] that '[n]ot every purpose beneficial to the community is a charitable purpose but only those which are within the equity of the preamble to the Statute of Elizabeth'. The doctrine also may linger in the related 'mischief' doctrine.

There is more than a trace of the doctrine in the response of the courts to certain protective legislation and, in more recent times, to taxation laws. The purpose of the *Bills of*

---

[94] Herman, 'The "Equity of the Statute" and *Ratio Scripta*: Legislative Interpretation among Legislative Agnostics and True Believers' (1994) 69 *Tulane Law Review* 535 at 538.

[95] Sutherland, *Statutes and Statutory Construction*, 5th edn (Singer (ed)), vol 2B, (1992 Rev of vol 2A), ch 54.

[96] Calabresi, 'A Common Law for the Age of Statutes' (1982) at 85–6; Blatt, 'The History of Statutory Interpretation: A Study in Form and Substance' (1985) 6 *Cardozo Law Review* 799 at 842–3.

[97] *Nelson v Nelson* (1995) 184 CLR 538 at 553–4. See *Craies on Statute Law*, 4th edn (1936) at 97–9; Wilberforce, *Statute Law* (1881) at 238–43; Sedgwick, *Statutory Construction*, 2nd edn (1874) at 311–16.

[98] *Incorporated Council of Law Reporting (Q) v Federal Commissioner of Taxation* (1971) 125 CLR 659 at 667.

Sale Act 1882 (UK) was to protect borrowers by requiring compliance with a prescribed form for bills given by way of security for payment of money by the grantor.[99] The question in the cases was whether documents fell within the statutory definition of bill of sale but the decisions showed a marked tendency 'to look through or outside the documents to the substance of the transaction'.[100]

Liability to capital gains tax under the *Finance Act* 1965 (UK) turned upon the existence of gains 'accruing to a person on the disposal of assets'.[101] The fiscal nullity doctrine developed by the House of Lords turns upon a distinction between 'tax mitigation' and 'unacceptable tax avoidance', the latter being 'in truth . . . no more than raids on the public funds at the expense of the general body of taxpayers'.[102] Certain tax avoidance schemes, whilst not shams, 'are nevertheless unacceptable because they embrace transactions which are not "real" disposals or do not generate "real" losses (or gains) and so are held not to attract certain fiscal consequences which would normally be attached to disposals or losses (or gains) under the relevant statute'.[103] The fiscal nullity doctrine (which is not a 'moral principle') is said essentially to arise from the construction of the relevant statute, not by judicial amendment of it.[104]

LEGISLATIVE INTENTION

Justice Scalia has given a depressing picture of the consequences in the United States of the modern obsession with the divination of legislative intention. His position is that legislative history being 'the statements made in the floor

[99] *Manchester, Sheffield, and Lincolnshire Railway Co v North Central Wagon Company* (1888) 13 App Cas 554 at 560–1.
[100] *Price v Parsons* (1936) 54 CLR 332 at 349.
[101] *Finance Act* 1965 (UK), s 19(1).
[102] *Ensign Tankers Ltd v Stokes* [1992] 1 AC 655 at 681.
[103] *Craven v White* [1989] AC 398 at 519; cf *John v Federal Commissioner of Taxation* (1989) 166 CLR 417 at 434–5.
[104] *Craven v White* [1989] AC 398 at 520.

debates, committee reports, and even committee testimony, leading up to the enactment of the legislation' should not be used 'as an authoritative indication of a statute's meaning'.[105] Justice Scalia's account of the pass to which matters have come in Supreme Court litigation should be repeated:[106]

> In the past few decades, however, we have developed a legal culture in which lawyers routinely—and I do mean routinely—make no distinction between words in the text of a statute and words in its legislative history. My Court is frequently told, in briefs and in oral argument, that 'Congress said thus-and-so'—when in fact what is being quoted is not the law promulgated by Congress, nor even any text endorsed by a single house of Congress, but rather the statement of a single committee of a single house, set forth in a committee report. Resort to legislative history has become so common that lawyerly wags have popularized a humorous quip inverting the oft-recited (and oft-ignored) rule as to when its use is appropriate: 'One should consult the text of the statute,' the joke goes, 'only when the legislative history is ambiguous.' Alas, that is no longer funny. Reality has overtaken parody. A few terms ago, I read a brief that *began* the legal argument with a discussion of legislative history and then continued (I am quoting it verbatim): 'Unfortunately, the legislative debates are not helpful. Thus, we turn to the other guidepost in this difficult area, statutory language.'[107]

That extreme has not been reached in other common law countries. However, there remain various curiosities in fashionable attitudes among Anglo-Australian lawyers.

---

[105] Scalia, *A Matter of Interpretation* (1997) at 29–30.
[106] Ibid., at 31.
[107] Brief for Petitioner at 21, *Jett v Dallas Independent School District* 491 US 701 (1989), quoted in *Green v Bock Laundry Machine Co* 490 US 504 at 530 (1989) (Scalia J concurring).

The first, and more apparent, is that expressed earlier this century by John Chipman Gray when he said:

> The fact is that the difficulties of so-called inter-
> pretation arise when the Legislature has had no
> meaning at all; when the question which is raised
> on the statute never occurred to it; when what
> the judges have to do is, not to determine what
> the Legislature did mean on a point which was
> present to its mind, but to guess what it would
> have intended on a point not present to its mind,
> if the point had been present.[108]

To repeat the words of Scalia J in the *Bank One Chicago Case*:

> Legislative history that does not represent the
> intent of the whole Congress is non-probative;
> and legislative history that does represent the
> intent of the whole Congress is fanciful.[109]

The second matter calling for comment is more fundamental. It concerns the respective spheres within which the
legislative and judicial branches operate. Perception here is,
one suspects, assisted by experience of a constitutional
structure with a formal separation of powers. That which is
binding (if it be a valid law) is the law as expressed, not as
it might have been expressed.

Meaning is not assimilated to legislative intention. The
former is not to be divined by the judicial branch from the
latter. The various aids to interpretation which now, since
Pepper v Hart,[110] are available at common law cannot be
determinative. In *Oncale v Sundowner Offshore Services Inc*,[111]
the question before the Supreme Court of the United States
was whether sexual harassment directed against the appellant by his male co-workers constituted 'discriminat[ion] . . .
because of . . . sex' as prohibited by Title VII of the *Civil
Rights Act of 1964*.[112] Scalia J delivered the opinion of a
unanimous Court and said:

---

[108] Gray, *The Nature and Sources of the Law*, 2nd edn (1926) at 172–3.
[109] *Bank One Chicago v Midwest Bank & Trust Company* 133 L Ed 2d 635 at 647
(1996).   [110] [1993] AC 593.   [111] 140 L Ed 201 (1998).
[112] 42 USC §2000e–2(a)(1).

As some courts have observed, male-on-male sexual harassment in the workplace was assuredly not the principal evil Congress was concerned with when it enacted Title VII. But statutory prohibitions often go beyond the principal evil to cover reasonably comparable evils, and it is ultimately the provisions of our laws rather than the principal concerns of our legislators by which we are governed.[113]

The point was made by Mason CJ, Wilson and Dawson JJ by saying that '[t]he words of [the second reading speech] of a Minister must not be substituted for the text of the law'.[114]

This follows the reasoning expressed by O W Holmes writing in 1899 in the *Harvard Law Review*. He said:

In the case of a statute, to turn from contracts to the opposite extreme, it would be possible to say that as we are dealing with the commands of the sovereign the only thing to do is to find out what the sovereign wants. If supreme power resided in the person of a despot who would cut off your hand or your head if you went wrong, probably one would take every available means to find out what was wanted. Yet in fact we do not deal differently with a statute from our way of dealing with a contract. We do not inquire what the legislature meant; we ask only what the statute means. In this country, at least, for constitutional reasons, if for no other, if the same legislature that passed it should declare at a later date a statute to have a meaning which in the opinion of the court the words did not bear, I suppose that the declaratory act would have no effect upon intervening transactions unless in a place and case where retrospective legislation was allowed. As retrospective legislation it would not work by way of construction except in form.[115]

[113] 140 L Ed 2d 201 at 207 (1998).
[114] *Re Bolton; Ex parte Beane* (1987) 162 CLR 514 at 518.
[115] 'The Theory of Legal Interpretation' (1899) 12 *Harvard Law Review* 417 at 419–20.

Those short term political considerations which appear often to drive the legislative process may lead to incoherent results. The final text of a Bill may be the product of a compromise made outside the legislative chambers and not fully disclosed by public debate in the legislature or elsewhere.[116] Again, there is a tendency of legislatures to pass laws which do not resolve difficult issues. Rather, in direct terms, the legislature remits the resolution of the issues on a case by case basis, with the listing of considerations (which between themselves may be incompatible)[117] to which the administrator or the court is to have regard. The result is legal norms which impose imperfect obligations, completed only by the resolution of each case. Family law and cognate legislation, which has displaced the confusions engendered by the application of constructive trusts law in this field, provide many examples. The consequence is that there is no true coalescence between the 'common law' and the statutory text.

Rather, there will be a wilderness of single instances. This will be the product of the exercise of discretions reposed by the legislature in the judicial or administrative decision-makers and, within the judicial hierarchy, of the restricted avenues in such cases for appeals and for judicial review. The doctrine of the 'equity of the statute' has returned, but with legislative imprimatur. In such situations, the search for a legislative intention may show no more than the desire to remit to the other branches of government the resolution of questions for which the legislature, in effect, declines responsibility itself to provide immediate answers.

On the other hand, statutes which on their face do speak directly to their subject may well be the result of compromise. This may have been achieved between contending factions within the government parties, between two legislative chambers and, particularly in narrowly divided

[116] Cf Barnes, 'Statutory Interpretation, Law Reform and Sampford's Theory of the Disorder of Law—Part Two' (1995) 23 *Federal Law Review* 77 at 93.

[117] See *Project Blue Sky Inc v Australian Broadcasting Authority* (1998) 72 ALJR 841; 153 ALR 490.

but powerful upper chambers in federal systems, between various political parties. Each of these may be responding wholly or partly to private representations by a range of interest groups. The resultant legislative process involves understandings, the existence and the terms of which cannot readily be made apparent to any court. The upshot is twofold. The first is that:

> [t]he 'purposive' school of statutory interpretation thus encounters the difficulty that it cannot accommodate the notion of 'factual matrix' as understood in modern authorities dealing with contractual interpretation.[118]

The second concerns the judicial function. The courts 'must respect the compromise embodied in the words chosen by [the legislature]'.[119] In *Rodriguez v United States*, the United States Supreme Court observed:

> [N]o legislation pursues its purposes at all costs. Deciding what competing values will or will not be sacrificed to the achievement of a particular objective is the very essence of legislative choice—and it frustrates rather than effectuates legislative intent simplistically to assume that *whatever* furthers the statute's primary objective must be the law.[120]

To a degree, this involves a reaffirmation of the importance of what once was cherished as the 'plain meaning' rule.[121] How is the existence of a legislative compromise to be ascertained? Judge Easterbrook urges the imposition by the courts upon legislatures of a duty of 'clear statements', so that unless 'the statute plainly hands courts the power to create and revise a form of common law, the domain of the statute should be restricted to cases anticipated by its

---

[118] *Brennan v Comcare* (1994) 50 FCR 555 at 573. See also Posner, *The Problems of Jurisprudence* (1990) at 276–7.

[119] *Mohasco Corp v Silver* 447 US 807 at 826 (1980).

[120] 480 US 522 at 525–6 (1987).

[121] Blatt, 'The History of Statutory Interpretation: A Study in Form and Substance' (1985) 6 *Cardozo Law Review* 799 at 839–40.

framers and expressly resolved in the legislative process'.[122]

Perhaps the most pervasive exercise of legal interpretation of laws produced by such compromises is by those charged with the administration of statutes pursuant to policies of the executive government. These policies are fluid, not static. They may be contrary to the policies of the common law. There is contrast between legislation as a fixed determination and as an element in such a dynamic process.

In *Re Drake (No 2)*,[123] in a passage which has often been cited, Sir Gerard Brennan dealt with the adoption by decision-makers (in this case, a Minister) of a general policy consistent with the duty of making individual decisions. He said:

> There are powerful considerations in favour of a Minister adopting a guiding policy. It can serve to focus attention on the purpose which the exercise of the discretion is calculated to achieve, and thereby to assist the Minister and others to see more clearly, in each case, the desirability of exercising the power in one way or another. Decision-making is facilitated by the guidance given by an adopted policy, and the integrity of decision-making in particular cases is the better assured if decisions can be tested against such a policy. By diminishing the importance of individual predilection, an adopted policy can diminish the inconsistencies which might otherwise appear in a series of decisions, and enhance the sense of satisfaction with the fairness and continuity of the administrative process.

The result may be that the policy as it stands from time to time in practice is determinative of the rights of citizens.

---

[122] Easterbrook, 'Statutes' Domains' (1983) 50 *University of Chicago Law Review* 533 at 544–5.   [123]   (1979) 2 ALD 634 at 640.

The widespread use by revenue authorities of 'rulings' which operate outside the court processes and without specific legislative foundation[124] is a significant instance of this. Moreover, both in the United Kingdom[125] and Australia,[126] there is authority that the courts should attach great weight to the interpretations adopted and applied by administrators of laws in 'specialist' fields, such as that of intellectual property.

In the United States, in *Chevron USA Inc v Natural Resources Defense Council, Inc*, the Supreme Court declared:

> When a court reviews an agency's construction of the statute which it administers, it is confronted with two questions. First, always, is the question whether Congress has directly spoken to the precise question at issue. If the intent of Congress is clear, that is the end of the matter, for the court, as well as the agency, must give effect to the unambiguously expressed intent of Congress. If, however, the court determines Congress has not directly addressed the precise question at issue, the court does not simply impose its own construction on the statute, as would be necessary in the absence of an administrative interpretation. Rather, if the statute is silent or ambiguous with respect to the specific issue, the question for the court is whether the agency's answer is based on a permissible construction of the statute.[127]

The issue in *Chevron* was whether delegated legislation went beyond its statutory source. The result appears to be that where statutes are ambiguous courts should accept any reasonable interpretation by the agency charged with their

---

[124] cf Pt IVAA of the *Taxation Administration Act* 1953 (Cth) and *CTC Resources NL v Commissioner of Taxation* (1994) 48 FCR 397.

[125] *In the Matter of Ford-Werke AG's Application for a Trade Mark* (1955) 72 RPC 191 at 194.

[126] *Registrar of Trade Marks v Muller* (1980) 144 CLR 37 at 41.

[127] 467 US 837 at 842–3 (1984) (footnotes omitted). The Opinion of the Court was delivered by Stevens J.

administration[128] and this is despite[129] apparent incompatibility with Marshall CJ's classic proposition that '[i]t is, emphatically, the province and duty of the judicial department, to say what the law is'.[130]

STATUTE AND NEW PRIVATE RIGHTS

Much statute law, over a long period, has been concerned to impose norms of conduct. Enforcement has been through the medium of the criminal law. On the civil side, judicial review may be available. The question has arisen whether, as a matter of private law and apart from remedies by way of judicial review, persons with an interest in that enforcement have their own civil remedy.[131] This usually (but not always, for injunctive relief may be available) is a pecuniary remedy.[132] The point is demonstrated by three related propositions, each of which illustrates the interaction, in a less than wholly satisfactory manner, between common law and statute. The propositions are difficult of application on a case by case footing. This reflects the failure to arrive at any generally accepted understanding of what is meant by reliance upon legislative intention.

First, there is the proposition formulated by Parke B in *Shepherd v Hills*[133] that wherever a statute creates a duty or

---

[128] Sunstein, 'Justice Scalia's Democratic Formalism', (1997) 107 *Yale Law Journal* 529 at 550–5.

[129] Monaghan, '*Marbury* and the Administrative State' (1983) 83 *Columbia Law Review* 1; Scalia, 'Judicial Deference to Administrative Interpretations of Law' [1989] *Duke Law Journal* 511 at 513–16; Davis and Pierce, *Administrative Law Treatise*, 3rd edn (1994), vol 1, §3.3.

[130] *Marbury v Madison* 5 US 137 at 177 (1803).

[131] Posner, 'Economics, Politics, and the Reading of Statutes and the Constitution' (1982) 49 *The University of Chicago Law Review* 263 at 275–80.

[132] The private right which is conferred by statute may attract protection by injunction, at least if it be of such a nature as to attract the intervention of the Court of Chancery: *Stevens v Chown* [1901] 1 Ch 894 at 904–5. See also *Duchess of Argyll v Duke of Argyll* [1967] Ch 302 at 345–7; *Fejo v Northern Territory* (1998) 72 ALJR 1442 at 1450, 1460; 156 ALR 721 at 733, 747–8.

[133] (1855) 11 Ex 55 at 67 [156 ER 743 at 747]. See also *Mallinson v Scottish Australian Investment Co Ltd* (1920) 28 CLR 66 at 70; *Middlesex County Sewerage Authority v National Sea Clammers Association* 453 US 1 at 14–15 (1981); *Roy v*

obligation to pay money then, unless the statute contains some provision to the contrary, an action will lie for its recovery. If the amount is liquidated the action in debt is appropriate.[134] Although the statute gives no particular method of enforcement, the obligation is treated none the less as a debt for the purposes of the common law action.[135]

The second proposition was propounded by Lord Tenterden CJ in *Doe v Bridges*.[136] It is that, where the statute creates a new right or imposes a new obligation (in *Bridges*, a land tax) with an associated statutory remedy to enforce it, performance cannot be enforced in any other manner. This is on the footing that the statute, upon its proper construction, having given the specific remedy, it 'thereby deprives the person who insists upon a remedy of any other form of remedy than that given by the statute'.[137] This doctrine has its counterpart in federal constitutional doctrines which pre-empt the operation of State law where the federal law 'covers the field'[138] or there is 'implied field pre-emption'.[139] Of course, the statute may create a right and give a remedy which is so inadequate that without more the right would be worthless. Thus, the copyright statute, 8 Anne c 19, gave to authors the sole right of reproduction of their works and attached certain penalties, yet it was held that had that been the only remedy 'the value of

---

Kensington and Chelsea and Westminster Family Practitioner Committee [1992] 1 AC 624 at 630, 649–50; *Trustees of the Dennis Rye Pension Fund v Sheffield City Council* [1998] 1 WLR 840; [1997] 4 All ER 747; *The Commonwealth v SCI Operations Pty Ltd* (1998) 192 CLR 285 at 313.

[134] *Hopkins v The Mayor, etc, of Swansea* (1839) 4 M & W 621 at 647 [150 ER 1569 at 1580]; affd (1841) 8 M & W 901 [151 ER 1306]. See also *The Commonwealth v SCI Operations Pty Ltd* (1998) 192 CLR 285 at 313.

[135] *Booth v Trail* (1883) 12 QBD 8 at 10.

[136] (1831) 1 B & Ad 847 at 859 [109 ER 1001 at 1005–6]. See also *Pasmore v Oswaldtwistle Urban Council* [1898] AC 387 at 394; *Josephson v Walker* (1914) 18 CLR 691 at 701; *Ex parte Carpathia Tin Mining Co Ltd* (1924) 35 CLR 552 at 554; *Thomson Australian Holdings Pty Ltd v Trade Practices Commission* (1981) 148 CLR 150 at 162–3; *Byrne v Australian Airlines Ltd* (1995) 185 CLR 410 at 425–6, 456–7; *Lonhro Ltd v Shell Petroleum Co Ltd [No 2]* [1982] AC 173 at 185–6; *Redrow Homes Ltd v Bett Bros plc* [1998] 2 WLR 198 at 204; [1998] 1 All ER 385 at 391–2.

[137] *Pasmore v Oswaldtwistle Urban Council* [1898] AC 387 at 394.

[138] *Ex parte McLean* (1930) 43 CLR 472 at 483.

[139] See *Rice v Santa Fe Elevator Corp* 331 US 218 at 230 (1947).

copyright would have been utterly destroyed'.[140] Hence, the common law gave a remedy by action on the case for the violation of the right created by the statute.[141] Again, the statutory right and remedy may be *sui generis*, with no common law or equitable analogue. In that event, the question does not arise.[142]

The third proposition is that, whilst in terms the statute creates no private right of action analogous to an action in debt or in tort for breach of its provisions, there is a civil remedy for what is generally described as breach of statutory duty.

The House of Lords recently has indicated that 'the fundamental question' is whether the legislature intended to confer upon the plaintiff a cause of action for breach of statutory duty'.[143] What this has come to involve is not 'the actual intention of the legislators' but that inference which arises 'on a balance of considerations, from the nature, scope and terms of the statute, including the nature of the evil against which it is directed, the nature of the conduct prescribed, the pre-existing state of the law, and, generally, the whole range of circumstances relevant upon a question of statutory interpretation'. These are the words of Kitto J in *Sovar v Henry Lane Pty Ltd*.[144]

There is a limited historical foundation for an emphasis upon 'intention'. In the last century, many of the statutes which gave rise to these questions were private acts for laying down of railways, water and gas supplies and other elements of modern infrastructure. The view that a private

[140] *Vallance v Falle* (1884) 13 QBD 109 at 111.

[141] *Beckford v Hood* (1798) 7 TR 620 at 627 [101 ER 1164 at 1167].

[142] For example, *Bailey v New South Wales Medical Defence Union Ltd* (1995) 184 CLR 399 at 446; cf *Issa v Hackney London Borough Council* [1997] 1 WLR 956; [1997] 1 All ER 999.

[143] *R v Deputy Governor of Parkhurst Prison; Ex parte Hague* [1992] 1 AC 58 at 159, 168–71. See also *Scally v Southern Health and Social Services Board* [1992] 1 AC 294 at 297, 307; *X (Minors) v Bedfordshire County Council* [1995] 2 AC 633 at 731–2; *O'Rourke v Camden London Borough Council* [1998] AC 188 at 192–3; Bennion, 'Codifying the Tort of Breach of Statutory Duty' (1996) 17 *Statute Law Review* 192.

[144] (1967) 116 CLR 397 at 405. See also *Sutherland Shire Council v Heyman* (1985) 157 CLR 424 at 482.

act had the nature of a compact between the promoters, the portion of the public directly interested in the matter and the legislature, brought with it considerations of intention.[145] In other circumstances, Sir Owen Dixon was critical of the reliance upon notions of intention in this area, saying that:

> As an examination of the decided cases will show, an intention to give, or not to give, a private right has more often than not been ascribed to the legislature as a result of presumptions or by reference to matters governing the policy of the provision rather than the meaning of the instrument. Sometimes it almost appears that a complexion is given to the statute upon very general considerations without either the authority of any general rule of law or the application of any definite rule of construction.[146]

The late Professor Fleming described this judgment as 'particularly noteworthy for its singular scepticism concerning the conventional judicial make-believe'.[147] To assimilate meaning to evinced intention is to attract the criticism by Holmes in the passage which I have set out above. To supply a text on the footing of an unimplemented intention must be an even odder procedure.

Chief Judge Posner has said of cases in which a remedy not fixed by the statute is discerned by the courts:

> This result is defensible only under the public interest theory of legislation. The absence of effective remedies implies to the interest group theorist that the group that procured the legislation lacked the political muscle to get an effective statute, and it is not the business of the courts to give an interest group a benefit that was denied by the legislature. Under this view, to imply a private right of

---

[145] *Byrne v Australian Airlines Ltd* (1995) 185 CLR 410 at 459–60; *Dartmouth College v Woodward* 4 Wheaton 518 at 627 [17 US 250 at 299] (1819); *Pennsylvania College Cases* 80 US 190 at 212–13 (1871).

[146] *O'Connor v SP Bray Ltd* (1937) 56 CLR 464 at 478.

[147] Fleming, *The Law of Torts*, 9th edn (1998) at 140, fn 174.

action is to intervene in the legislative struggle on
the side of one interest group, overriding oppos-
ing groups that had managed to thwart the enactment of an effective statute.[148]

This criticism would not have attracted the New Zealand
Court of Appeal when dealing with *Baigent's Case*.[149] The
New Zealand Bill of Rights Act 1990 (NZ) 'affirmed' (s 2) the
Bill of Rights set out in ss 8–27 but stipulated (s 4) that no
enactment was to be held to be impliedly repealed or
revoked or to be in any way invalid or ineffective by reason
of its 'inconsistency' with any provision of the Bill of
Rights. Nor, on that ground, was any court to decline to
apply any enactment. No new remedy was specified in the
statute. However, the Court of Appeal held that 'effective
remedies must be available under the New Zealand Act for
violations of affirmed rights'.[150] This was so even though a
proposed remedies clause[151] did not find its way into the
enacted law. The Court concluded that 'it was not
Parliament's intention that the only remedies for infringement of rights should be those at common law'.[152]

The concentration upon legislative 'intention' also char-
acterizes the decisions of the United States Supreme Court
and other federal courts dealing with the implication of a
private right of action for violation of regulatory regimes
established by federal statute. In 1975, in *Cort v Ash*, the
Court stated a four part test:

First, is the plaintiff 'one of the class for whose
especial benefit the statute was enacted' ... that
is, does the statute create a federal right in favor
of the plaintiff? Second, is there any indication of
legislative intent, explicit or implicit, either to

[148] Posner, 'Economics, Politics, and the Reading of Statutes and the
Constitution' (1982) 49 *The University of Chicago Law Review* 263 at 278–9.
[149] *Simpson v Attorney-General* [1994] 3 NZLR 667.
[150] [1994] 3 NZLR 667 at 677.
[151] Clause 25 had read: '*Enforcement of guaranteed rights and freedoms.* Anyone
whose rights or freedoms as guaranteed by this Bill of Rights have been infringed
or denied may apply to a court of competent jurisdiction to obtain such remedy
as the court considers appropriate and just in the circumstances.'
[152] [1994] 3 NZLR 667 at 699.

> create such a remedy or to deny one? . . . Third, is
> it consistent with the underlying purposes of the
> legislative scheme to imply such a remedy for the
> plaintiff? . . . And finally, is the cause of action
> one traditionally relegated to state law, in an area
> basically the concern of the States, so that it
> would be inappropriate to infer a cause of action
> based solely on federal law?[153]

The result in *Cort v Ash* was a holding that a law which
prohibited, under criminal sanction, corporate contributions
to presidential and vice-presidential candidates did not create
a private right of action available to the shareholders of a
corporation which contravened the statute. More recently, the
Supreme Court has said that the 'most important inquiry' is
'whether Congress intended to create the private remedy
sought by the plaintiffs'.[154] Earlier, it had found that a private
right of action existed where the legislative history (including
the debates in Congress) demonstrated a clear congressional
intent to do so, albeit and paradoxically, that intent had not
been translated into direct action.[155]

Another view, which Professor Atiyah considered but in
the end did not accept,[156] was that the results in the cases
were achieved as creative efforts 'by way of analogy to, or
extension of, the statute', in order to integrate the private
law of obligations with the penal provisions which usually
enforced the regulatory scheme in question.

THE CONSTITUTIONAL DIMENSION

Somewhat different questions arise where the norm which
is infringed is constitutionally entrenched. The constitution

---

[153] 422 US 66 at 78 (1975). See Williams, 'Statutes as Sources of Law Beyond
Their Terms in Common-Law Cases' (1982) 50 *The George Washington Law Review*
554 at 576–80.

[154] *Suter v Artist M* 503 US 347 at 364 (1992).

[155] *Cannon v University of Chicago* 441 US 677 at 694–703 (1979). See Davis and
Pierce, *Administrative Law Treatise*, 3rd edn (1994), vol 3, §18.5; Grey, 'Make
Congress Speak Clearly: Federal Preemption of State Tort Remedies' (1997) 77
Boston University Law Review 559, fn 16.

[156] 'Common Law and Statute Law' (1985) 48 *Modern Law Review* 1 at 12–14.

may upon a fair reading create new remedies for those complaining of infringement of its provisions by those in public authority.[157] Sub-section 24(1) of the Canadian Charter of Rights and Freedoms[158] states:

> Anyone whose rights or freedoms, as guaranteed by this Charter, have been infringed or denied may apply to a court of competent jurisdiction to obtain such remedy as the court considers appropriate and just in the circumstances.

This authorizes an award of damages, including exemplary damages.[159] In the United States, although the Constitution itself contains no provision such as s 24(1) which directly creates such a cause of action, an action for damages is allowed to a limited and controversial extent[160] for violation of constitutional rights. The action (the *Bivens* action[161]) is limited to violations by officials and employees of the federal government, not by the federal government itself or federal agencies.[162] Nor does the *Bivens* action apply against State or local officials acting under colour of State law.[163] This implied cause of action is to be understood against the limited waiver in the *Federal Torts Claims Act of 1946*[164] and the application of the *Civil Rights Act of 1871*[165] to deprivation of federal rights by State or local officials acting under colour of State law. In a sense, the *Bivens* action was implied to fill a legislative gap.[166]

---

[157] See, for example, *Maharaj v Attorney-General of Trinidad and Tobago (No 2)* [1979] AC 385.

[158] Being Pt I of the *Constitution Act* 1982, which is Sched B to the *Canada Act* 1982 (Imp).   [159] *Crossman v The Queen* [1984] 1 FC 681 at 694–5.

[160] Davis and Pearce, *Administrative Law Treatise*, 3rd edn (1994), vol 3, §19.5; Hart and Wechsler, *The Federal Courts and the Federal System*, 4th edn (1996) at 866–77.

[161] *Bivens v Six Unknown Named Agents of Federal Bureau of Narcotics* 403 US 388 (1971).

[162] *Federal Deposit Insurance Corporation v Meyer* 510 US 471 at 473, 484–5 (1994).

[163] *Bivens v Six Unknown Named Agents of Federal Bureau of Narcotics* 403 US 388 (1971); *Federal Deposit Insurance Corporation v Meyer* 510 US 471 (1994).

[164] 28 USC §§1346, 2671–80.   [165] 42 USC §1983.

[166] *Federal Deposit Insurance Corporation v Meyer* 510 US 471 at 485 (1994).

On the other hand, in Australia the High Court jurisprudence sees the common law as antecedent to the Constitution. The view there is that in respect of executive action in excess of constitutional authority or in contravention of a constitutional prohibition the remedy is that under the common law in respect of tortious or other wrongful acts.[167] This reflects the view that it does not necessarily follow that, because the Constitution confers an immunity in respect of certain activity by individuals or imposes restraints upon legislative or executive power, the Constitution itself confers a 'right' with a constitutional remedy upon a personal cause of action.[168]

However, the situation in the European Union has developed in the other direction. In certain circumstances, member states may be liable to provide reparation for damage sustained by individuals by reason of breach by other individuals and by member States of European law (including directives).[169] It will be convenient to refer further to related issues of federalism in the third of these lectures.

---

[167] *James v The Commonwealth* (1939) 62 CLR 339 at 369–70; *McClintock v The Commonwealth* (1947) 75 CLR 1 at 19; *Nelungaloo Pty Ltd v The Commonwealth* (1942) 85 CLR 545 at 567–8; *Northern Territory v Mengel* (1995) 185 CLR 307 at 350–3, 372–3.

[168] *Kruger v The Commonwealth* (1997) 190 CLR 1 at 46–7, 93, 124–6, 146–8.

[169] *Three Rivers District Council v Bank of England (No 3)* [1996] 3 All ER 558; *Brasserie du Pêcheur SA v Federal Republic of Germany [Factortame No 4]* [1996] QB 404 at 506; Craig, 'Once More unto the Breach: the Community, the State and Damages Liability' (1997) 113 *Law Quarterly Review* 67.

Lecture Two—
Equity Follows the Law

Contrary to the tenor of the title to this lecture, in various senses the relationship between law and equity may be seen as the law taking the lead from equity.

There is force in the statement by Professor Laycock: 'The war between law and equity is over. Equity won.'[1]

The remedy of the common injunction gave equitable remedies that primacy which, at the doctrinal level, was represented by the prevalence given by s 25(11) of the *Judicature Act* 1873 (UK) to the rules of equity where there was any conflict or variance between them and the rules of the common law with respect to the same matter.

The Judicature system, to a large and still insufficiently appreciated degree, also provided a modern law of procedure which was equitable in derivation. In the United States federal courts, that modern procedure was introduced in the 1938 Federal Rules of Civil Procedure. This represented the triumph of the views of Pound and others that it was the formalism of the common law writ system which hindered the just application of substantive law and its adjustment to modern circumstances.[2] The constitutionally mandated retention of the jury trial in many civil cases tried in federal and State courts in the United States—a

[1] Laycock, 'The Triumph of Equity' (Summer 1993) 56 *Law and Contemporary Problems* 53 at 53.

[2] Subrin, 'How Equity Conquered Common Law: The Federal Rules of Civil Procedure in Historical Perspective' (1987) 135 *University of Pennsylvania Law Review* 908 at 944–9.

matter to which I refer in the next lecture—is a notable exception to the derivation of modern procedure from equity.

This lecture treats a maxim which, by indicating the restraint in various matters of doctrine, perhaps contributed to that triumph. It is convenient to commence by saying a little concerning the maxims of equity.

The maxims have been described by Mason CJ and McHugh J as 'summary statement[s] of ... broad theme[s] which underlie[] equitable concepts and principles'.[3] Those themes are concerned with more than the values of the counting-house. Rather, often they direct attention to individual circumstances, to exceptions to rules and to the attaining of justice in the particular case, especially between a range of parties with different interests in the one subject-matter. Hence, perhaps, the irritation with equitable institutions, doctrines, and remedies (particularly the fiduciary principle) of those who see law as but an adjunct of one or other of fashionable economic theories, including the theories identified with 'economic rationalism'.[4]

The focus of this lecture is upon a precept of equity which is apparently technical in nature, though not always in its implementation. The precept that 'equity follows the law' encourages the notion that what now are regarded as the 'core subjects' of the common law of obligations, contract and tort, have a greater antiquity than is the case. Yet to a significant degree, both are products of nineteenth-century decisions and treatises, whereas the guiding principles of equity are older, perhaps considerably so.

In his Introduction to vol 1 of *Lord Nottingham's Chancery Cases*,[5] Yale demonstrates that the principle reflected in the

---

[3] *Corin v Patton* (1990) 169 CLR 540 at 557.

[4] See Langbein and Posner, 'Social Investing and the Law of Trusts', (1980) 79 *Michigan Law Review* 72; Easterbrook and Fischel, 'Corporate Control Transactions' (1982) 91 *Yale Law Journal* 698 at 715–35; Cooter and Freedman, 'The Fiduciary Relationship: Its Economic Character and Legal Consequences' (1991) 66 *New York University Law Review* 1045; Easterbrook and Fischel, 'Contract and Fiduciary Duty' (1993) 36 *Journal of Law and Economics* 425; Duggan, 'Is Equity Efficient?' (1997) 113 *Law Quarterly Review* 601.

[5] (1954) 73 Selden Society at lxii.

maxim 'he who seeks equity must do equity' 'was of the greatest force in the court [of Chancery] at least as early as Lord Nottingham's time'. So also the 'pervasive' principle that equality is equity.[6]

A member of Lincoln's Inn, writing at the beginning of the nineteenth century, could identify 'that system of artificial and methodized reason called equity . . . which, with all its imperfections, may be characterized as one of the most noble and exalted efforts of human intellect'.[7] In the preface to vol 11 of his Reports, published in 1858, Hare wrote of the then recent changes in Chancery procedure. He praised the improvements which the legislature had made and, as to substance, he went on to urge the following:

> Equity, amongst us, has always had too much vitality within it—has been too conversant with action, and too inquisitive into motive—to become the mere creature of artifice or the arbitrary expression of authority. The judge or the counsel may rest upon or take shelter under some precedent, whilst they are looking beyond it to a principle, either implanted in the conscience or founded on a more or less comprehensive argument or sense of utility. No equitable doctrine which has not its root in an enlightened morality can be venerable or lasting.[8]

On the other hand, the conceptual development of the common lawyers was cramped by an organizational method which 'was procedural rather than substantive, by remedies rather than by rights', so that 'a plaintiff's claim might fail solely because it could not be framed within the existing structure of remedies'.[9] It was this 'remedial

---

[6] (1954) 73 Selden Society at lxiii.

[7] Cooper, *A Treatise of Pleading on the Equity Side of the High Court of Chancery* (1813) at xxxviii. The views to similar effect of other eighteenth-century writers are collected in Lieberman, *The Province of Legislation Determined: Legal theory in eighteenth-century Britain*, (1989) at 74–5.

[8] Hare's Reports, (1858), vol 11 at xxviii.

[9] Ibbetson, 'Unjust Enrichment in England before 1600' in Schrage (ed), *Unjust Enrichment: The Comparative Legal History of the Law of Restitution* (1995), 121 at 122.

formalism', with attendant development of fictions,[10] which was 'a central feature of the common law'.[11] Contemplation of that state of affairs may encourage a triumphalist view of the historical mission of equity. This has been neatly described by a Canadian scholar as:

> [A] dire story of the tough, unyielding common law where conscience had no home; a legal system almost wholly devoid of the ability to deal with human problems; a play in which only one act—that of the Court of Chancery with performers of humanistic learning and equity— kept alive the burning fires of justice in a deeply authoritarian and repressive world.[12]

What is more significant for present purposes is the link between equitable doctrines and the precepts or ideas as to the arrangement of human affairs which support them. The point may be illustrated by the judgment of Windeyer J in *Uren v John Fairfax & Sons Pty Ltd*.[13] His Honour referred to the acceptance by Lord Devlin of the proposition that exemplary damages 'originated just 200 years ago in the cause célèbre of John Wilkes and the North Briton in which the legality of a general warrant was successfully challenged'.[14] Windeyer J said he took leave to doubt whether the 'exemplary principle' was only of such recent appearance and continued:

> However, like any attempt to trace the lineage of an idea, much depends on how far you wish to go back and how much certainty you demand in the connecting links.[15]

[10] A point made by Dixon CJ in *Commissioner for Railways (NSW) v Cardy* (1960) 104 CLR 274 at 285. The doctrine of 'general reliance' may be a recent example of a fiction which is doctrinal rather than remedial: *Stovin v Wise* [1996] AC 923 at 953–5; *Pyrenees Shire Council v Day* (1998) 192 CLR 330 at 387–8.

[11] Getzler, 'Patterns of Fusion' in Birks (ed), *The Classification of Obligations* (1997) 157 at 169.

[12] Knafla, 'Conscience in the English Common Law Tradition' (1976) 26 *University of Toronto Law Journal* 1 at 1.

[13] (1966) 117 CLR 118.

[14] *Rookes v Barnard* [1964] AC 1129 at 1221–2.

[15] (1966) 117 CLR 118 at 152.

In equity, the lineage of an idea may be quite clear and its persistence through changing circumstances all the more readily explicable.

INNOVATION

In *Kleinwort Benson Ltd v Lincoln City Council*,[16] Lord Browne-Wilkinson spoke of the rejection of the declaratory theory of precedent but of the presence of its progeny, 'the retrospective effect of a change made by judicial decision'. In the debate to which that decision contributes, much turns upon the meaning given to the notion of retrospectivity.

Yale showed[17] that Lord Nottingham 'may be said to be a pioneer in equity in providing reasons for his rules or even providing new reasons for old rules' and that he initiated many new rules in equity, there being 'no fiction, as is sometimes claimed for the common law, that the principles of equity have existed from time immemorial'. Sir Anthony Mason has said that equity, 'having its origins in ecclesiastical and natural law, made no secret of its evolutionary development'.[18]

Those who have stressed (even without accepting in any extreme form the declaratory theory) the gradual evolution of common law principles may overlook the very different characteristic of equity to which Sir Anthony Mason referred. The point was made by Sir George Jessel MR in the well-known passage in *In re Hallett's Estate; Knatchbull v Hallett*[19]. The Master of the Rolls said:

> [I]t must not be forgotten that the rules of Courts of Equity are not, like the rules of the Common Law, supposed to have been established from time immemorial. It is perfectly well known that they have been established from time to time— altered, improved, and refined from time to time.

[16] [1998] 3 WLR 1095 at 1100; [1998] 4 All ER 513 at 518.
[17] (1954) 73 Selden Society at cxxi–cxxii.
[18] Mason, 'The Impact of Equitable Doctrine on the Law of Contract' (1998) 27 *Anglo-American Law Review* 1 at 3.   [19] (1879) 13 Ch D 696.

In many cases we know the names of the Chancellors who invented them. No doubt they were invented for the purpose of securing the better administration of justice, but still they were invented. Take such things as these: the separate use of a married woman, the restraint on alienation, the modern rule against perpetuities, and the rules of equitable waste.[20]

To that one may add, as Mr Hackney recently pointed out, the recognition that some of the duties of the trustee of an express trust are not fiduciary in nature,[21] and the comparatively late development of fiduciary duties imposed upon persons who were not classified as trustees.[22]

The notion of regular development of the common law from time immemorial has been put in proper perspective by Professor Brian Simpson. Writing on the subject of the contribution of Holmes to the doctrine of tort law, Professor Simpson states:

> By the time Holmes became interested in the subject, there had been tort actions for some six hundred years. During that long period, juries had been deciding cases, thousands and thousands of them in which plaintiffs sought damages for wrongs, cases brought before them by formal procedures, chiefly, but not exclusively, actions of trespass and trespass on the case. But before the nineteenth century there was very little in the way of an abstract body of substantive law which could be called the principles of tort law. Such reported cases as had been

[20] Ibid., at 710.

[21] Hackney, 'More than a trace of the old philosophy' in Birks (ed), *The Classification of Obligations* (1997) 123 at 143. See also *Breen v Williams* (1996) 186 CLR 71 at 137.

[22] Hackney, 'More than a trace of the old philosophy' in Birks (ed), *The Classification of Obligations* (1997) at 143–4. See also Waters, 'Banks, Fiduciary Obligations and Unconscionable Transactions' (1986) 65 *Canadian Bar Review* 37 at 43–5. The result has been a challenge to legal taxonomy which still is to be answered by the courts: see De Mott, 'Fiduciary Obligations under Intellectual Siege: Contemporary Challenges to the Duty to be Loyal' (1992) 30 *Osgoode Hall Law Journal* 471.

> generated by all this litigation were classified, for
> example by compilers of abridgements of cases,
> but until well into the nineteenth century there
> was very little in the way of a treatise literature
> purporting to set out the supposed principles
> underlying the farrago of cases.[23]

He goes on to emphasize that in the nineteenth century matters of private common law, once treated as issues of fact to be left to juries, were coming to be governed by judge-controlled law.[24] The result for private common law generally was that 'in effect, it was being invented'.[25]

The common law of obligations matured in its modern form during an age of *laissez-faire*, the influence of which may be seen in the development of such doctrines as those of common employment and contributory negligence. In such a *Zeitgeist*, some established equitable principles were not readily accommodated. The attitude of equity to time stipulations[26] and the jurisdiction to relieve against penalties and forfeitures were something of an affront to the doctrine of freedom of contract. The same might be said of cases in which transactions have been held in substance to be mortgages despite their being cast in another form.[27] Indeed, to a common lawyer such as Lord Bramwell, the equity of redemption itself gave offence. As late as 1892, in *Salt v Marquess of Northampton*, his Lordship said:

> Whether it would not have been better to have
> held people to their bargains, and taught them by
> experience not to make unwise ones, rather than
> relieve them when they had done so, may be

[23] Simpson, 'The Elusive Truth About Holmes' (1997) 95 *Michigan Law Review* 2027 at 2035–6.

[24] A point developed by Dr. Getzler in his essay, 'Patterns of Fusion' in Birks (ed) *The Classification of Obligations* (1997) 157 at 187–90.

[25] Simpson, 'The Elusive Truth About Holmes' (1997) 95 *Michigan Law Review* 2027 at 2036.

[26] As to which there may be developing a split between Privy Council and Australian authority: see *Union Eagle Ltd v Golden Achievement Ltd* [1997] AC 514 at 521–3; 'Notes', (1997) 113 *Law Quarterly Review* 385.

[27] See, for example, *Gurfinkel v Bentley Pty Ltd* (1966) 116 CLR 98; *In re Bond Worth Ltd* [1980] Ch 228.

doubtful. We should have been spared the
double condition of things, legal rights and equitable rights, and a system of documents which
do not mean what they say. But the piety or love
of fees of those who administered equity has
thought otherwise. And probably to undo this
would be more costly and troublesome than to
continue it.[28]

The nineteenth-century decisions and treatises gave us
the law of contract, not a law of contracts. This law grew, not
from any fundamental propositions or general theory found
in the body of English law, but largely around the action of
assumpsit. The structure which was developed by Anson
and Pollock,[29] with its emphasis upon offer and acceptance,
intention to create legal relations, consideration, and privity,
is still with us, at least in the law schools. However, legislative intervention in a number of areas, be it carriage of goods
by sea, insurance, consumer credit, or consumer purchases,
has tended to produce a law of contracts.

Tort has developed rather differently. We are often
reminded, most recently by Professor Hepple,[30] that negligence has 'overshadowed all other torts, encroached on
their territory, and sometimes overwhelmed them'. It also
has encroached on what once would have been thought the
exclusive sphere of contract. Negligence may have
provided, at last, a law of tort in place of the law of torts. Yet
negligence lacks coherence, both in a formal sense (the
insufficiency of criteria such as 'reasonable foreseeability'
and 'proximity') and in a functional sense (the lack of agreement as to the ends or purposes which it serves).

One suspects that in significant measure this stems from
two causes. For much of this century, in Anglo-Australian
law there has been an avoidance of too explicit a consideration of the ends sought to be served by the imposition of

---

[28] [1892] AC 1 at 18–19.

[29] See Simpson, 'Innovation in Nineteenth Century Contract Law' (1975) 91
Law Quarterly Review 246 at 250–65.

[30] 'Negligence: The Search for Coherence' (1997) 50 *Current Legal Problems* 69
at 69.

tortious liability. Further, in the many and disparate cases in which non-contractual liability in damages was enforced before the nineteenth century, there was an emphasis upon procedure rather than doctrine. The latter is a latecomer to the law of tort.

Hence the statement by Professor Simpson:

> Indeed, the whole idea of trying to discover the common law principle of liability in pre-nineteenth-century law seems to me to be wholly misconceived; from time to time the question surfaced in legal discussion, as it did in 1466 [in *The Case of Thorns*[31]], but it was never resolved because it did not need to be resolved. The expansion of substantive law in the nineteenth century meant that questions that were previously left to lay common sense became the subject of legal doctrine. They now required a legal answer.
>
> It is not easy to see why this happened; the common law had managed for centuries without definitions of insanity for criminal law, principles for assessing damages in contract, or legal definitions of negligence. But whatever the explanation, the underlying idea must have been that the scope of legal liability ought, in a system based on the ideal of the rule of law, to be determined by law, not by jury discretion.[32]

On the other hand, the modern law of restitution, as it develops in England, is rich in theory. Perhaps this is because it develops unconstrained by what appears to be a rather barren conceptual past. Professor Burrows[33] has said that 'as the "implied contract" theory was a fiction, deeper reasoning must always have been guiding the courts', which 'have throughout been applying the principle of unjust enrichment, albeit at times in an unadventurous and stunted

---

[31] *Hulle v Orynge* (1466) Y B 6 Edw IV, fol 7, pl 18.
[32] Simpson, 'The Elusive Truth About Holmes' (1997) 95 *Michigan Law Review* 2027 at 2037–8.
[33] 'Restitution: Where Do We Go From Here?' (1997) 50 *Current Legal Problems* 95 at 97, reprinted Burrows, *Understanding the Law of Obligations* (1998) 99 at 101.

way'. However, I suspect Professor J H Baker and Professor Langbein are nearer the mark. The former concludes that, by the time of Lord Mansfield, 'the common law provided restitutionary remedies in a number of situations, but still had no coherent theory to explain them'.[34] The latter gives as his thesis that the law of unjust enrichment is, in a sense, historically contingent upon the development of the law of obligations, particularly of contract, saying:

> [o]nly when the nineteenth-century legal systems had worked out the contours of the modern law of contract was it possible to see the range of unjust enrichment problems that contract law—honest contract law—could not solve.[35]

Thus, the detailed historical analysis of quantum meruit conducted by the High Court in *Pavey & Matthews Pty Ltd v Paul*[36] apparently was undertaken to base that action upon a footing independent of the old pleading system whence it came.[37]

On the other hand, at least from the time of Lord Nottingham, the Chancellors had striven to provide rational justification for the particular applications of principle. However, they had been faced by the dilemma that what is just as between the parties will not necessarily be so if it be erected into a principle of general application. The point has been reiterated as follows by Lord Browne-Wilkinson:

> [B]y using trusts and fiduciary duties as vehicles to produce justice, the Court does not only adjust personal liability but at the same time recognizes

---

[34] Baker, 'The History of Quasi-Contract in English Law' in Cornish *et al.* (eds), *Restitution: Past, Present and Future*, (1998), 37 at 53. See also Ibbetson, 'Unjust Enrichment in England before 1600' in Schrage (ed), *Unjust Enrichment: The Comparative Legal History of the Law of Restitution* (1995), 121 at 148.

[35] Langbein, 'The Later History of Restitution' in Cornish *et al.* (eds), *Restitution: Past, Present and Future*, (1998), 57 at 59. See also Dietrich, *Restitution: A New Perspective* (1998) at 27–9.

[36] (1987) 162 CLR 221 (HC), (1985) 3 NSWLR 114 (NSWCA).

[37] Sheahan, 'Use and Misuse of Legal History: Case Studies from the Law of Contract, Tort and Restitution' (1998) 16 *Australian Bar Review* 280 at 290–7; Jackman, *The Varieties of Restitution*, (1998) at 73–6.

48 Lecture Two

the existence of property rights ... which can
and do operate to the detriment of third parties
who are in real terms without blame.[38]

The historical differences between law and equity reflect
that tension between the goal of certainty and consistency,
which appears to come from the application of rigid rules,
and the goal of justice in the individual case, which continues to characterize judicial decision-making. Sir Anthony
Mason summed up that historical difference by saying that
equity and common law 'reflected different value
systems'.[39] Sir Anthony added that there was 'another side
to equity' exemplified by artificial rules of construction
applied to wills.

Professor Reynolds has rightly observed that a study of
rivalry between principles, as opposed to a study of their
interaction and interrelation, is unlikely to be productive
for the study of what should be one coherent system of
law.[40] That coherent system will allow for and represent the
product of continued interaction and interrelation between
law and equity. The doctrines and remedies of equity are
not 'frozen in time'.[41] The development since *Saltman
Engineering Co Ltd v Campbell Engineering Co*[42] of the law
with respect to breach of confidence and the rise of the anti-
suit injunction indicate the contrary and illustrate the vitality of equity.

Again, the continued significance of equitable remedies
upon the development of the substantive law of contract
should not be underestimated. I doubt if many now would
accept the statement made by Holmes in 1881:

The only universal consequence of a legally binding promise is, that the law makes the promisor

---

[38] 'Equity in a Fast Changing World' [1996] *New Zealand Law Conference* 170 at
176.
[39] Mason, 'The Impact of Equitable Doctrine on the Law of Contract' (1998) 27
Anglo-American Law Review 1 at 3.
[40] Reynolds, 'Contract and Tort: The View from the Contract Side of the
Fence' (1993) 5 *Canterbury Law Review* 280 at 281.
[41] Cf *Canson Enterprises Ltd v Boughton & Co* [1991] 3 SCR 534 at 580.
[42] (1948) 65 RPC 203.

pay damages if the promised event does not
come to pass. In every case it leaves him free
from interference until the time for fulfilment has
gone by, and therefore free to break his contract if
he chooses.[43]

For example, Judge Friendly pointed out in *Thyssen, Inc v
SS Fortune Star*,[44] that the theory that 'a contract is simply a
set of alternative promises either to perform or to pay
damages for nonperformance' would be sufficient explanation for a rule that punitive damages are not recoverable for
a breach of contract, at least where there is no concurrent
liability in tort. Nevertheless, his Honour went on, 'a good
many other [explanations] have been offered', including the
burden that punitive damages would place upon the
doctrine of efficient breach.

Earlier, in the passage set out above, Holmes conceded
that 'in some instances equity does what is called
compelling specific performance' but said that, with respect
to a promise to convey land within a certain time, 'a court
of equity is not in the habit of interfering until the time has
gone by, so that the promise cannot be performed as made'.
This confirmed to Holmes his thesis that the law 'never
interferes until a promise has been broken, and therefore
cannot possibly be performed according to its tenor'. In this
Holmes was in error. The true position was stated by
Williams, Fullagar and Kitto JJ in *Turner v Bladin*.[45] Their
Honours said:

> In our opinion proceedings for the specific
> performance of a contract which is of such a kind
> that it can be specifically enforced can be
> commenced as soon as one party threatens to
> refuse to perform the contract or any part thereof
> or actually refuses to perform any promise for
> which the time of performance has arrived. The
> court can then make a decree that the contract

---

[43] Lecture VIII, 'Contract—II Elements' in *The Common Law*, (1881), reprinted
in Novick (ed), *The Collected Works of Justice Holmes* (1995), vol 3, 263 at 269.

[44] 777 F 2d 57 (1985).

[45] (1951) 82 CLR 463. See also *Hasham v Zenab* [1960] AC 316 at 329–30.

ought to be specifically performed and carried
into execution, and can so mould its decree and
order such inquiries, accounts and other
proceedings under the decree as may be necessary to carry into effect all the promises of both
parties whether they are presently performable
or are only performable in the future.[46]

This reasoning, expressed in relation to a particular equitable remedy, has influenced the formulation of contractual
doctrine. The point was made by Windeyer J in *Coulls v
Bagot's Executor and Trustee Co Ltd*.[47] By way of implied
rebuke to Holmes J, Windeyer J declared:[48]

The primary obligation of a party to a contract is
to perform it, to keep his promise. That is what
the law requires of him. If he fails to do so, he
incurs a liability to pay damages. That however
is the ancillary remedy for his violation of the
other party's primary right to have him carry out
his promise. It is, I think, a faulty analysis of legal
obligations to say that the law treats a promisor
as having a right to elect either to perform his
promise or to pay damages. Rather, using one
sentence from the passage from Lord Erskine's
judgment which I have quoted above[49], the
promisee has 'a legal right to the performance of
the contract'. Moreover, we are concerned with
what Fullagar J once called 'a system which has
never regarded strict logic as its sole inspiration.'[50]

[46] (1951) 82 CLR 463 at 472.
[47] (1967) 119 CLR 460. See also *Lep Air Services v Rolloswin Investments Ltd*
[1973] AC 331 at 346–7 per Lord Diplock.
[48] (1967) 119 CLR 460 at 504. These observations were repeated by Lord
Pearce in *Beswick v Beswick* [1968] AC 58 at 91, and by Brennan J in *Trident General
Insurance Co Ltd v McNiece Bros Pty Ltd* (1988) 165 CLR 107 at 139.
[49] In *Alley v Deschamps* (1806) 13 Ves Jun 225 at 227–8 [33 ER 278 at 279], Lord
Erskine said: 'This Court assumed the jurisdiction upon this simple principle; that
the party had a legal right to the performance of the contract; to which right the
Courts of Law, whose jurisdiction did not extend beyond damages, had not the
means of giving effect.'
[50] *Tatham v Huxtable* (1950) 81 CLR 639 at 649.

So, in *Co-operative Insurance Society Ltd v Argyll Stores (Holdings) Ltd*,[51] Lord Hoffmann stated that 'the purpose of the law of contract is not to punish wrongdoing but to satisfy the expectations of the party entitled to performance'. In that case, a decree of specific performance (for a period which might not end until 2014) of the covenants in a lease of a supermarket would have been unjust because the remedy (under the shadow of 'heavy and expensive' contempt applications)[52] would have enabled the plaintiff to secure in money terms more than the performance due to it. The plaintiff would have been put in a position to extract for its release by the defendant a sum greater than its actual damnification.[53]

THE MAXIM

That the maxim or precept 'equity follows the law' is an incomplete statement of the relationship between them is apparent from what seems to be its first recorded appearance in the Chancery reports. Cary (whose reports cover the period 1557–1602) had it as follows:

> Conscience never resisteth the law, nor addeth to it, but only where the law is directly in itself against the law of God, or the law of Reason; for in other things, *Equitas sequitur legem*.[54]

St German had written to similar effect in Ch XVI of *The First Dialogue between Doctor and Student*,[55] saying that equity followed the law 'in al partyculer cases where ryght and Iustyce requyreth'. In the sense used by Cary,

---

[51] [1998] AC 1 at 15.

[52] In Australia, charges of contempt of this nature must be proved beyond reasonable doubt: *Witham v Holloway* (1995) 183 CLR 525.

[53] The possible consequences of refusal of specific performance on such grounds are canvassed by Professor Tettenborn, 'Absolving the Undeserving: Shopping Centres, Specific Performance and the Law of Contract' [1998] *The Conveyancer* 23 at 33–6. See also *Patrick Stevedores Operations No 2 Pty Ltd v Maritime Union of Australia [No 3]* (1998) 72 ALJR 873 at 893–4; 153 ALR 643 at 669–70.   [54] *Anonymous* (nd) Cary 11 [21 ER 6].

[55] Selden Society, *St German's Doctor and Student* (1974), vol 91 at 97.

conscience appears to have 'consisted of those collected habits which had been shaped through the exercise of [man's] reason'.[56] Hence the notion of 'reasonableness'.[57] By this means, these writers sought to show how equity might mitigate the law without abrogating it. Here also is the basis of the doctrine of the equity of the statute, to which reference was made in the first lecture. The legislator is taken to have intended the interpretation of the statute to allow for exceptions when circumstances demanded. To follow the letter of the law at the expense of its spirit then would be 'to thwart legislative intent and in effect to corrupt the law'.[58]

The statement that whilst equity follows the law it does so neither 'slavishly nor always' was made by Cardozo CJ in the New York Court of Appeals in *Graf v Hope Bldg Corporation*[59]. He said (omitting citations):

> Equity declines to treat a mortgage upon realty as a conveyance subject to a condition, but views it as a lien irrespective of its form. Equity declines to give effect to a covenant, however formal, whereby in the making of a mortgage, the mortgagor abjures and surrenders the privilege of redemption. Equity declines in the same spirit, to give effect to a covenant, improvident in its terms, for the sale of an inheritance, but compels the buyer to exhibit an involuntary charity if he is found to have taken advantage of the necessities of the seller. Equity declines to give effect to a covenant for liquidated damages if it is so unconscionable in amount as to be equivalent in its substance to a provision for a penalty. One could give many illustrations of the traditional and unchallenged exercise of a like

[56] Knafla, 'Conscience in the English Common Law Tradition' (1976) 26 *University of Toronto Law Journal* 1 at 5.

[57] Vinogradoff, 'Reason And Conscience in Sixteenth-Century Jurisprudence' (1908) 24 *Law Quarterly Review* 373 at 379.

[58] Behrens, 'An Early Tudor Debate on the Relation between Law and Equity' (1998) 19 *The Journal of Legal History* 143 at 157.

[59] 171 NE 884; 254 NY 1 (1930).

> dispensing power. It runs through the whole
> rubric of accident and mistake. Equity follows
> the law, but not slavishly nor always. If it did,
> there could never be occasion for the enforce-
> ment of equitable doctrine.[60]

The preference of equity for substance over form and for
intention over the method of its expression, the concern of
equity at the unconscientious exercise of legal rights, the
imposition of terms upon the grant of equitable relief in aid
of legal rights and the weapon of the common injunction (to
enforce the prevalence now given to equity by the
Judicature system) underline the point made by
Cardozo CJ. The contrast between the basal notions which
animate the common law on the one hand and equity on
the other has been restated by Lord Millett, with reference
to contemporary commercial life. He wrote:[61]

> The common law insists on honesty, diligence,
> and the due performance of contractual obliga-
> tions. But equity insists on nobler and subtler
> qualities: loyalty, fidelity, integrity, respect for
> confidentiality, and the disinterested discharge
> of obligations of trust and confidence. It exacts
> higher standards than those of the market place,
> where the end justifies the means and the old
> virtues of loyalty, fidelity and responsibility are
> admired less than the idols of 'success, self-
> interest, wealth, winning and not getting
> caught'.[62]

It is the concern of equity with standards of probity and
good conscience, the adaptability of equitable doctrine to
changing circumstances and the discretionary nature of
equitable relief which, to use words of Sir Anthony Mason,
'stand in marked contrast to the more rigid formulae
applied by the common law and equip it better to meet the

---

[60] 171 NE 884 at 886–7; 254 NY 1 at 9 (1930).
[61] Millett, 'Equity's Place in the Law of Commerce' (1998) 114 *Law Quarterly
Review* 214 at 216.
[62] Sacks, *The Politics of Hope* (1997) at 179.

needs of the type of liberal democratic society which has evolved in the twentieth century'.[63] An example is the adaptation by Mason J himself of equitable principles to deal with the protection of governmental secrecy.[64] Another is the development in the constitutional law of the United States of the 'structural injunction' to implement desegregation.[65]

An instance of the limits which attend the development of equitable doctrine is the refusal in *Breen v Williams*[66]—the medical records case—to reinvent tort law as equitable compensation for breach of fiduciary duty. The English Court of Appeal recently has stressed the fundamental distinctions, rooted in legal history, between legal and equitable rights, titles and interests. In *MCC Proceeds Inc v Lehman Bros International (Europe)*,[67] Hobhouse LJ emphasized the character of legal remedies, which, deriving from legal rights, are not discretionary and may impose strict liabilities upon innocent third parties, and contrasted equitable rights and remedies. The award of damages in conversion to a plaintiff with a beneficial interest in personal property but without an immediate right to possession would be a new species of fusion fallacy. It would impermissibly seek to combine 'a strict legal remedy with a mere equitable right'.[68]

What has been said above indicates that to insist upon clarity of thought and an understanding of the conceptual roots of living equitable doctrine is rather more than to

[63] Mason, 'The Place of Equity and Equitable Remedies in the Contemporary Common Law World' (1994) 110 *Law Quarterly Review* 238 at 239. Lord Browne-Wilkinson has written in similar terms: 'Equity in a Fast Changing World', [1996] *New Zealand Law Conference* 170 at 171–2.

[64] *The Commonwealth of Australia v John Fairfax & Sons Ltd* (1980) 147 CLR 39 at 52. See also the observations by McHugh JA in *AG (UK) v Heinemann Publishers Pty Ltd* (1987) 10 NSWLR 86 at 191.

[65] *Brown v Board of Education of Topeka* 349 US 294 at 300 (1955); *Milliken v Bradley* 433 US 267 at 279–81 (1977); Tribe, *American Constitutional Law*, 2nd edn. (1988), §16–18, §16–19.   [66] (1996) 186 CLR 71.

[67] [1998] 4 All ER 675 at 701.

[68] [1998] 4 All ER 675 at 701. See also at 691 per Mummery LJ and see further Tettenborn, 'Trust Property and Conversion: An Equitable Confusion' (1996) 55 *Cambridge Law Journal* 36.

indulge, as La Forest J put it, 'a misguided sense of orderliness'.[69] The insistence which I prefer still allows for the force in the observation that:

> Where the common law once premised the availability of a remedy on the plaintiff's capacity to satisfy the requirements of a writ, and equity once acted openly on the conscience of the defendant, the mediation of these countervailing criteria of justice in and *through* the person of the judge constitutes a primary problematic of late modern jurisprudence.[70]

EQUITY IN AN AGE OF STATUTES

The immediate further concern of this lecture is with equity in an age of statutes. Here what is to be followed is not precedent which is indicative of the judge-made law, but a text which has legislative paramountcy. Several issues arise.

The vast jurisdiction now vested in the courts with respect to rights and obligations solely created by statute frequently requires the exercise of judicial discretion. The reasons which move legislatures to enact laws of this nature were considered in the first of these lectures. To the exercise of such jurisdiction the 'equity mind' will more readily adapt.

Statute may adopt general law principles and institutions as elements in a new regime. An example is the 'trust' for 'statutory purposes'.[71] A statutory body in which a fund is vested may be styled as a 'Trust' or may be given by its constituent statute the investment powers of trustees. Nevertheless, contributors to the fund lack the beneficial

---

[69] *Canson Enterprises Ltd v Boughton & Co* [1991] 3 SCR 534 at 573.

[70] Chesterman, 'Beyond Fusion Fallacy: The Transformation of Equity and Derrida's "The Force of Law" ' (1997) 24 *Journal of Law and Society* 350 at 357 (footnote omitted).

[71] *Bathurst City Council v PWC Properties Pty Ltd* (1998) 72 ALJR 1470 at 1479–83; 157 ALR 414 at 426–31.

interest of an ordinary *cestui que trust*.[72] The statute may include an express statement that the body it creates is not bound by the law relating to the administration of trust funds by trustees. However, in other respects this body may still have the character of a trustee in the ordinary sense of moneys held by it.[73]

> In such ways the legislature may create entities which have some but not all of the characteristics of a trust. In each case the true construction of the law determines the degree of the analogy.[74]

Another example concerns the jurisdiction in equity to set aside dealings which are the product of unconscientious conduct. Australian legislation has developed from this basis by authorizing review of contracts whose terms are harsh or oppressive.[75] That is to say, the legislation goes beyond unconscientious conduct.

Two particular matters require further attention. The first is the taking of new statutory rights and obligations as the objects upon which equitable doctrines and remedies operate. In *Mayfair Trading Co Pty Ltd v Dreyer*,[76] Dixon CJ made the fundamental point:

> Whatever remedies at law are given by or arise in consequence of the statute may, of course, be pursued by the party unconditionally. But something more would be required before a court of equity intervened on equitable grounds and so went further in point of remedy than the statute provided.

For example, how does contribution operate in respect of statutory rights and obligations? May there be relief in equity against forfeiture of such rights? May there be a

---

[72] *Fouche v The Superannuation Fund Board* (1952) 88 CLR 609 at 640; *Superannuation Fund Investment Trust v Commissioner of Stamps (SA)* (1979) 145 CLR 330 at 353–4, 362–4.

[73] *Registrar of the Accident Compensation Tribunal v Federal Commissioner of Taxation* (1993) 178 CLR 145 at 161–8.

[74] *Wik Peoples v Queensland* (1996) 187 CLR 1 at 197.

[75] *Trade Practices Act* 1974 (Cth), ss 52A, 52AA, 52AB.

[76] (1958) 101 CLR 428 at 450.

vendor's lien? When will an injunction be granted in aid of (*a*) the observance by the defendant of a statutory prohibition or (*b*) the protection of a statutory right of the plaintiff? Reference has been made to the latter situation in the first lecture. The former entangles equity's attitudes to enforcement of the criminal law and to standing.

The second matter concerns equitable intervention in, as it were, the opposite direction. Here the question is whether equity will restrain the unconscientious use of statutory rights, privileges and immunities or otherwise mollify the consequences of the operation of the statute. For example, legislation may prescribe particular formalities for the essential validity of, or for the proof of, *inter vivos* or testamentary dispositions. Certain transactions may require registration upon a public register. In the face of the prescription of a statute which appears to cover the field (for example, as to registered land title), what is 'sufficient to justify [a] court [of equity] in breaking in upon an act of parliament'[77] so as to 'interfere to prevent the machinery of an Act of Parliament being used by a person to defend equities which he himself has raised'?[78] Why should it ever be unconscientious to rely on legal rights or immunities conferred by statute? More may be involved here than the application of principles of statutory interpretation. This is because results are produced which differ from those apparently dictated by the ordinary and natural meaning of statutory provisions.[79]

I further consider these two matters in turn.

STATUTORY RIGHTS AND OBLIGATIONS AS THE OBJECT OF EQUITABLE
DOCTRINES AND REMEDIES

The operation of equity in this field may be illustrated by reference to the doctrine of contribution. Equity acts upon

[77] An expression used by Lord Harwicke LC in *Hine v Dodd* (1741) 2 Atk 275 at 276 [26 ER 569 at 570].
[78] *Phillips v Martin* (1890) 11 NSWLR (L) 153 at 158; appr *Wilson v McIntosh* [1894] AC 129 at 134.
[79] Rajak, 'Equity v Statute' in Goldstein (ed), *Equity and Contemporary Legal Developments* (1992) 100 at 113.

the basis that 'equality is equity'[80] and to prevent
inequitable exercise of legal rights.[81] Equity intervenes to
forestall expenditure with later contribution as much as to
provide for recovery of contribution after expenditure has
been made. Thus, a surety may enforce a claim to contribution as soon as the creditor has acquired a right of immediate payment from the surety.[82] The plaintiff and the
contributor must be subjected to co-ordinate liability.
Contribution through sureties and insurers are examples
where the source of the coordinate liability is contractual.
However, the source or a source of liability may be statutory.

Armstrong v Commissioner of Stamp Duties[83] concerned
s 25 of the *Gift Duty Assessment Act* 1941 (Cth). This
provided that gift duty constituted a debt due to the
Crown by the donor and the donee jointly and severally.
The New South Wales Court of Appeal held that there was
a right of contribution between donor and donee and that
it was no answer that the co-ordinate liability had been
imposed by statute rather than created by voluntary acts
of the respective parties.[84] Subsequently, in *Spika Trading
Pty Ltd v Harrison*,[85] Giles J considered legislation which
imposed criminal liability upon directors of companies
which incurred debts when there were reasonable
grounds to expect that the companies would be unable to
meet their debts and which also rendered the directors
jointly and severally liable for the payment of those debts.
Giles J held that the statute, in its civil aspect, gave rise to
co-ordinate liabilities which called for contribution
between the directors and that this was so notwithstanding the legislative imposition of concurrent criminal liabilities.[86]

The doctrine of contribution applied in these cases, not
by reason of an implication in the statutes themselves, but

---

[80] *Scholefield Goodman and Sons Ltd v Zyngier* [1986] AC 562 at 571.
[81] *Mahoney v McManus* (1981) 180 CLR 370 at 387.
[82] Ibid., at 376.   [83] [1967] 2 NSWR 63.
[84] Ibid., at 69.   [85] (1990) 19 NSWLR 211.
[86] Ibid., at 217.

because the statutes created liabilities which had characteristics answering the criteria for equitable intervention. In
such a situation the question had been whether the statute
in terms or by necessary implication excluded the equity
jurisdiction.[87]

Once it is accepted that the doctrine of contribution may
operate where the relevant liabilities are imposed by statute
rather than generated by institutions of the general law
such as contract (as with sureties) and the law of trusts (as
with express trustees),[88] it is no objection that one co-ordinate liability is based in statute and another in the general
law. The criterion is whether the liabilities are 'of the same
nature and same extent'.[89] In *BP Petroleum Development Ltd
v Esso Petroleum Co Ltd*,[90] an oil tanker owned by Esso had
damaged a jetty in the Shetlands. By statute, Esso was liable
to the port authority for the damage to the jetty, and by
contract with the port authority BP was liable to it for the
same damage. BP had paid the authority. Lord Ross held
that BP might recoup half of its outgoings from Esso, it not
being to the point that the common obligations to the
authority arose as to BP from contract and as to Esso from
statute.

In *Eagle Star Insurance Co Ltd v Provincial Insurance Plc*[91],
the liability of each insurer to pay the amount of a judgment
recovered against the insured by a third party arose solely
under statute and not under their respective contracts of
insurance. The Privy Council held that 'this distinction in
the source of the liability does not by itself justify any depar-
ture from the normal approach'.[92] In a sense there were two
levels of obligation, that of the insured under the contracts
and that of the third party under the statute. Each insurer
would, on the facts, have been entitled to repudiate liability

---

[87] See *Webster v The Bread Carters' Union of NSW* (1930) 30 SR (NSW) 267 at 276
(injunction); *Bank of New South Wales v City Mutual Life Assurance Society Ltd* [1969]
VR 556 at 559 (marshalling); cf *Bristol City Council v Lovell* [1998] 1 WLR 446 at
453–4; [1998] 1 All ER 775 at 782–3 (statutory injunction).

[88] Special considerations may apply where contribution is sought between
constructive trustees or between express and constructive trustees.

[89] *Caledonian Railway Co v Colt* (1860) 3 Macq 833 at 844.

[90] 1987 SLT 345. [91] [1994] 1 AC 130. [92] Ibid., at 139.

to the insured. With respect to the statutory obligations of the two insurers, their Lordships concluded that '[n]o distinction should be made in relation to their respective positions and accordingly they should each contribute equally to the amount payable to [the third party]'.[93]

It may be noted that in *Eagle Star* the statutory obligation to the third party only arose if the insurer was then entitled to avoid or cancel the policy or had done so.[94] Accordingly, it is difficult to see how the two levels of obligation would have had any concurrent or reciprocal operation. However, the submissions of counsel do not appear to have been framed in that way. Rather, the Privy Council suggested that, if both insurers had been liable at least in part to the insured under the contracts, the consequence would have been that 'they should contribute to their statutory liability [to the third party] in accordance with their respective liability to the person insured for the loss'.[95]

There will be no equity calling for contribution where the statutory liability is primary in nature and that of guarantors or others sharing coordinate liability under the general law is secondary.[96] This is because contribution is founded on the principle that equality is equity and there is no room for application of the doctrine to parties not placed 'on the same level of liability'.[97]

Statutory systems of registered title give rise to particular problems. For example, the strict formal requirements imposed by the Imperial Shipping Acts of George III[98] had the consequence that specific performance could not be decreed of an informal agreement for the sale of a ship.[99] Likewise, it was held that legislation did not permit the enforcement of any resulting trust otherwise arising by the

---

[93] [1994] 1 AC 130 at 142.
[94] See the text of s 12 of the statute, set out at [1994] 1 AC 130 at 136–7.
[95] Ibid., at 141.
[96] *Street v Retravision (NSW) Pty Ltd* (1995) 56 FCR 588 at 599.
[97] *Scholefield Goodman and Sons Ltd v Zyngier* [1986] AC 562 at 575.
[98] 26 Geo III c 60, 34 Geo III c 68.
[99] *Hibbert v Rolleston* (1792) 3 Bro CC 571 [29 ER 705]; *Thompson v Leake* (1815) 1 Madd 39 [56 ER 16]; *Brewster v Clarke* (1816) 2 Mer 75 [35 ER 869].

payment of purchase money.[100] The legislation left no scope
for equity to relieve against the consequences of accident,
mistake or even fraud.[101]

These authorities were relied upon in early decisions
construing the Torrens system of land title by registration.
They were not followed. It was held that there was no analogy between the two registration systems. The point was
made as follows in an early decision of the Supreme Court
of South Australia. In *Cuthbertson v Swan*, it was said:[102]

> [T]he great policy of the Shipping Acts to which
> everything had to be subservient, and which
> required a particular mode of transfer and regis-
> tration in order to afford the means of discovering
> the true owners of British ships, in order that none
> but British subjects should have interest in them,
> and which compelled the Courts—even in the
> absence of prohibitive words—to declare that there
> could be no transfer of equitable as distinguished
> from legal interests in British ships, or in a form not
> recognised by the Acts, has no counterpart in the
> Real Property Act, except as to the protection of
> purchasers from adverse claims, which can be
> sufficiently effected without prohibiting the exis-
> tence of trusts enforceable, except as against
> purchasers, and transferable like any other
> description of equitable estates or interests in real
> property not under the provisions of the Act. There
> is nothing in the policy of the Real Property Act
> which renders it necessary that trusts should not
> exist, or that contracts for the sale of land should
> not be enforced so long as a person acquiring a title
> by transfer as a purchaser is protected from
> adverse claims, estates, or interests.[103]

---

[100] *Ex parte Yallop* (1808) 15 Ves Jun 60 at 66–7 [33 ER 677 at 680]; *Chasteauneuf
v Capeyron* (1881) 7 App Cas 127 at 131; *Garrett v L'Estrange* (1911) 13 CLR 430 at
435; *Barry v Heider* (1914) 19 CLR 197 at 214–16; *Nelson v Nelson* (1995) 184 CLR 538
at 564–5, 605–6. See also *Preston v Preston* [1960] NZLR 385 at 405; *Orr v Ford* (1989)
167 CLR 316 at 328.

[101] *Thompson v Leake* (1815) 1 Madd 39 at 43–4 [56 ER 16 at 17].

[102] (1877) 11 SALR 102 at 111–12.

[103] See also *Barry v Heider* (1914) 19 CLR 197 at 214–16.

Over a long period, legislation in the Australian colonies and States has provided for the grant by the Crown of an extensive and varied range of what might collectively be described as pastoral tenures. Many of these are *sui generis* but they take their place within the legal order. These interests may be the object of rights and obligations created *inter partes* and supported by the law of contract. For breach of a contractual obligation to deal in one of these statutory interests, a remedy in the nature of specific performance may be available.[104]

There are applicable to such interests and dealings therein equitable doctrines which apply to 'common law transactions of an analogous character'.[105] In *Minister for Lands and Forests v McPherson*,[106] Mahoney JA gave as examples equitable doctrines relating to release or waiver and acquiesence. Depending upon the particular characteristics attached by statute to the interest in question, there may be an equity to relief against forfeiture of that interest.[107] The exercise by the executive of a statutory power with respect to the granting of such interests may be attended by obligations to afford procedural fairness and, if so, equity, by injunction, may restrain eviction of the plaintiff pending the determination of an application for a further grant.[108]

On the other hand, in *Davies v Littlejohn*,[109] the High Court held that, in respect of a conditional purchase under the *Crown Lands Consolidation Act* 1913 (NSW), the Crown did not have a vendor's lien for the instalments of purchase money not yet due. The relationship under the statute of the Crown and the grantee was not sufficiently analogous of that between vendor and purchaser whereby, on

---

[104] *Butts v O'Dwyer* (1952) 87 CLR 267; *McWilliam v McWilliams Wines Pty Ltd* (1964) 114 CLR 656 at 660–1; *Brown v Heffer* (1967) 116 CLR 344 at 349–50.

[105] *Minister for Lands and Forests v McPherson* (1991) 22 NSWLR 687 at 713.

[106] (1991) 22 NSWLR 687 at 713.

[107] *Attorney-General of Victoria v Ettershank* (1875) LR 6 PC 354 at 370; *McPherson v Minister for Natural Resources* (1990) 22 NSWLR 671 at 682–3; affd *Minister for Lands and Forests v McPherson* (1991) 22 NSWLR 687 at 697–703, 713–15.

[108] *State of Queensland v Litz* [1993] 1 Qd R 343 at 349–51.

[109] (1923) 34 CLR 174.

contract, the purchaser became in equity the owner of the
land and the position of the vendor in equity was protected
by the lien.[110]

A particular difficulty has arisen where statute extin-
guishes or renders unenforceable the legal obligations of a
party who then seeks equitable relief which goes further in
point of remedy than that for which the statute has
provided. The laws against usury and later money-lending
legislation have been the source of much illustrative litigation. This legislation might render void securities which
appeared good on their face. A receiver and manager might
enter into possession under such an instrument. Would
equity order delivery up and cancellation of the instruments or enjoin the trespass by the receiver?

The answer given by Dixon CJ in *Mayfair Trading Co Pty
Ltd v Dreyer*[111] was that equity would intervene where there
was 'some ground, some particular situation, giving an
equity to the party to the form of relief sought', being a
remedy beyond that provided by the statute. Thus, 'a
continuing trespass to property, particularly the seizure of a
business, if without legal authority, might well be considered sufficient in itself to justify the intervention of the
court of equity with its special remedy of an injunction'.[112]

On the other hand, an equity entitling a party to delivery
up and cancellation of instruments, or to an injunction
against suing at law upon them, 'must rest on other
grounds'; the declaration by the legislature that a particular
transaction is illegal or void 'does not in itself warrant a
court of equity in improving upon or adding to what the
legislature has done'.[113] However, Dixon CJ reasoned in
Mayfair Trading that rescission of the entire transaction and
restitution of the parties so far as might be to the situation
they initially occupied, would be equitable relief appropriate to the situation in which the statute placed the
parties.[114] By the plaintiff's submitting to the condition on

---

[110] Ibid., at 183, 186–8, 195.
[111] (1958) 101 CLR 428 at 450–1.   [112] Ibid., at 451.
[113] Ibid.   [114] Ibid.

its part to effect restitution *in integrum*, the plaintiff might make out an equitable title to relief.[115] A borrower who sought rescission and alleged that securities were void under the money-lending legislation but did not offer to repay the moneys borrowed with legal interest was seeking equity but not doing equity.[116]

In *Lodge v National Union Investment Company, Limited*,[117] Parker J granted relief to a borrower from a transaction with an unregistered money-lender by ordering delivery up by the lender of certain bills of exchange and conveyances and a policy of life insurance. However, it was made a condition of the relief that it should be upon repayment by the borrower to the lender of the balance of their loan moneys and some premiums the latter had paid.[118] It was the situation created by the legislation which gave the borrower the right to be restored to his former position but the borrower's equity rested upon something more than the legal right or immunity given by the legislation, namely upon the offer of restitution.

In *Kasumu v Baba-Egbe*,[119] the borrower brought an action seeking delivery up of mortgage documents and the Privy Council rejected the contention of the money-lender that such relief, being equitable, should be granted only on terms of repayment of the money. The Privy Council held that the imposition of such a requirement as a condition of equitable relief would constitute a claim in respect of a transaction within the very terms of the statutory prohibition.[120] This stated that the money-lender 'shall not be entitled to enforce any claim in respect of any transaction in relation to which the default shall have been made'. Neither as a condition of relief nor otherwise could the borrower be required to account for or to restore to the lender the loan moneys remaining unrepaid. This would have been to contradict the terms of the statute or, at least, as McHugh J later put it:

---

[115] Ibid. at 451–2.
[116] See *Maguire v Makaronis* (1997) 188 CLR 449 at 475–7, 499–500.
[117] [1907] 1 Ch 300.   [118] Ibid., at 312.
[119] [1956] AC 539.   [120] Ibid., at 550–1.

To grant relief to the borrower on terms that he or she restore to the moneylender any benefits obtained from that person would be contrary to the policy of the legislation.[121]

Speaking with respect to the Statute of Frauds, Story declared:

[W]e may apply the remark that the proper juris-diction of Courts of Equity is to take every one's act according to conscience, and not to suffer undue advantage to be taken of the strict forms of law or of positive rules.[122]

One approach is to identify the relief sought by the plaintiff or the grounds upon which relief is sought as lying outside the mischief to which the statute in question is directed. Examples are provided by the decisions of Lord Hardwicke LC upon the statute 7 Anne c 20. This required registration of certain dealings with interests in realty situated in the County of Middlesex. Deeds and conveyances, if not registered in accordance with the statute, were to be 'adjudged fraudulent and void against any subsequent purchaser or mortgagee for valuable consideration'. In *Le Neve v Le Neve*,[123] Lord Hardwicke LC looked to the preamble of the statute which referred to 'prior and secret conveyances, and fraudulent incumbrances' and treated 'the intention of the act' as being '[p]lainly to secure subsequent purchasers, and mortgagees against *prior secret conveyances, and fraudulent incumbrances*'.[124] He continued:

Where a person had no notice of a prior conveyance, there the registring [*sic*] his subse-quent conveyance shall prevail against the prior,

---

[121] *Nelson v Nelson* (1995) 184 CLR 538 at 617. See also *Pavey & Matthews Pty Ltd v Paul* (1987) 162 CLR 221 at 226, 261–2, 269–70.

[122] Story, *Equity Jurisprudence* (1835), vol 1, §331.

[123] (1748) 3 Atk 646 [26 ER 1172].

[124] (1748) 3 Atk 646 at 651 [26 ER 1172 at 1174].

but if he had notice of a prior conveyance, then
that was not a secret conveyance by which he
could be prejudiced.

The enacting clause says, *That every such deed
shall be void against any subsequent purchaser or
mortgagee, unless the memorial thereof be registered,
&c*, that is, it gives them the legal estate, but it
does not say, that such subsequent purchaser is
not left open to any equity, which a prior
purchaser or incumbrancer may have, for he can
be in no danger where he knows of another
incumbrance, because he might then have
stopped his hand from proceeding.

. . .

[I]t would be a most mischievous thing, if a
person taking the advantage of the legal form
appointed by an act of parliament, might, under
that, protect himself against a person who had a
prior equity, *of which he had notice*.[125]

This was in an age when the doctrine of the equity of the
statute, to which I have referred in the first lecture, was given
fairly free rein to limit the literal operation of legislation.

On the other hand, where a statute provides that no
proceedings shall lie for recovery or enforcement of a
contract of loan and supporting securities, the lender cannot
assert in its favour the equitable doctrine of subrogation so
as to 'keep alive' the unpaid vendor's lien over the land
purchased by the borrower with the proceeds of the loan.[126]
This is said to be because, even if the terms of the legislation
are not of sufficient width to deny that remedy, to allow it
would 'enable the court to express a policy of its own in
regard to moneylending transactions which would be in
direct conflict with the policy of the [legislation] itself'.[127]

---

[125] Ibid., at 651–2 [26 ER 1172 at 1174–5]. See also *Hine v Dodd* (1741) 2 Atk 275
[26 ER 569]; Fonblanque, *A Treatise of Equity*, (1793), vol 1 at 23.

[126] *Orakpo v Manson Investments Ltd* [1978] AC 95; cf *Banque Financière de la Cité
v Parc (Battersea) Ltd* [1998] 2 WLR 475 at 487–8; [1998] 1 All ER 737 at 749; Barrett,
'Unjust enrichment' (1998) 72 *Australian Law Journal* 357.

[127] [1978] AC 95 at 115 per Lord Edmund-Davies; cf *Tinsley v Milligan* [1994] 1
AC 340; *Nelson v Nelson* (1995) 184 CLR 538.

At one stage, the cases developing the doctrine of part performance as an answer to a defence of unenforceability, based upon s 4 of the Statute of Frauds, applied similar reasoning to that of Lord Hardwicke LC upon the statute of Anne. However, by the time of *Maddison v Alderson*,[128] Lord Selborne LC was able to say:

> That equity [of part performance] has been stated by high authority to rest upon the principle of fraud: 'Courts of Equity will not permit the statute to be made an instrument of fraud.' By this it cannot be meant that equity will relieve against a public statute of general policy in cases admitted to fall within it . . . [T]his summary way of stating the principle (however true it may be when properly understood) is not an adequate explanation, either of the precise grounds, or of the established limits, of the equitable doctrine of part performance.[129]

Lord Selborne's reformulation of principle was that, where the plaintiff relies upon the doctrine of part performance:

> the defendant is really 'charged' upon the equities resulting from the acts done in execution of the contract, and not (within the meaning of the statute) upon the contract itself. If such equities were excluded, *injustice of a kind which the statute cannot be thought to have had in contemplation would follow.*[130]

For all that had happened with statutory interpretation since *Le Neve v Le Neve* was decided in 1748, the phrase 'cannot be thought to have had in contemplation' might have been used by Lord Hardwicke.

In *Maddison v Alderson*, Lord Selborne gave as an example of equities resulting from acts done in the execution of a contract those that would arise where a parol contract had

---

[128] (1883) 8 App Cas 467.   [129] Ibid., at 474.
[130] Ibid., at 475 (emphasis added). See also at 489 per Lord Blackburn.

been completely performed on both sides as to everything except conveyance: the purchase money had been paid, the purchaser had been put into possession and this had been followed by expenditure by the purchaser in improvements to the land and the granting of leases by the purchaser. In such circumstances, if the vendor refused a conveyance and sought to eject the purchaser, the matter would have 'advanced beyond the stage of contract' and the equities which had arisen out of that stage could not 'be administered unless the contract [was] regarded'.[131] The Lord Chancellor emphasized that s 4 of the Statute of Frauds 'does not avoid parol contracts, but only bars the legal remedies by which they might otherwise have been enforced'.[132]

It will be recalled that in *Dillwyn v Llewelyn*,[133] a leading case upon 'proprietary estoppel', Lord Westbury LC had said that the case in hand was 'somewhat analogous to that of verbal[134] agreement not binding originally for the want of the memorandum in writing signed by the party to be charged, but which becomes binding by virtue of the subsequent part performance'. Further, specific performance may be decreed, apparently independently of the doctrine of part performance, where the lack of writing is due to fraud or dishonesty of the defendant involving representations upon which the plaintiff has relied.[135]

Finally, I refer to some consequences of the repeal of the modern representative of s 4 of the Statute of Frauds (s 40 of the *Law of Property Act* 1925 (UK)) by s 2(8) of the *Law of Property (Miscellaneous Provisions) Act* 1989 (UK). This reform may have removed that to which the doctrine of part performance was a response.[136] Nevertheless, the new

---

131 Ibid., at 476.   132 Ibid., at 474.

133 (1862) 4 De G F & J 517 at 521–2 [45 ER 1285 at 1286].

134 Presumably his Lordship meant 'oral'.

135 *Maxwell v Lady Mountacute* (1719) Prec Ch 526 [24 ER 235]; *Wakeham v Mackenzie* [1968] 1 WLR 1175 at 1182; [1968] 2 All ER 783 at 788; cf *Wood v Midgley* (1854) 5 De G M & G 41 at 45 [43 ER 784 at 786].

136 The material parts of s 2 are:

'(1) A contract for the sale or other disposition of an interest in land can

regime does not exhaust the potentialities of the principles of estoppel.[137] In addition, the general considerations involved in Lord Selborne's reasoning in *Maddison v Alderson* as to the equities upon which the defendant may be charged are of general significance.

One result of the new legislation, as expounded in *United Bank of Kuwait plc v Sahib*[138], is that in England the deposit of title deeds by way of security no longer creates a valid equitable mortgage or charge. The Court of Appeal held that the equitable charge created by deposit of title deeds was 'contract-based'[139] and thus controlled by s 2 of the 1989 statute.

This outcome may be compared with that in the earlier Court of Appeal decision.[140] There the assignment for value of property not then in existence attached to the after acquired property notwithstanding the supervening bankruptcy (and discharge) of the assignor. The assignment was 'contract-based' but the contract had been discharged before the assignor acquired the asset. Therefore, the ground for

---

only be made in writing and only by incorporating all the terms which the parties have expressly agreed in one document or, where contracts are exchanged, in each.

'(2) The terms may be incorporated in a document either by being set out in it or by reference to some other document.

'(3) The document incorporating the terms or, where contracts are exchanged, one of the documents incorporating them (but not necessarily the same one) must be signed by or on behalf of each party to the contract.

. . .

'(5) . . . nothing in this section affects the creation or operation of resulting, implied or constructive trusts.

'(6) In this section—

"disposition" has the same meaning as in the Law of Property Act 1925;

"interest in land" means any estate, interest or charge in or over land or in or over the proceeds of sale of land.

. . .

'(8) Section 40 of the Law of Property Act 1925 (which is superseded by this section) shall cease to have effect.'

[137] Pettit, 'Farewell Section 40' [1989] *The Conveyancer* 431 at 442–3; Critchley, 'A *Via Media* for Estoppel and Third Parties?' [1998] *The Conveyancer* 502.

[138] [1997] Ch 107, noted (1997) 113 *Law Quarterly Review* 533.

[139] [1997] Ch 107 at 128. [140] *In re Lind* [1915] 2 Ch 345.

equitable intervention could not have been the susceptibility of a subsisting contract to a decree of specific performance.[141] Equity intervened on a different basis. It regarded as done that which ought to be done because the assignor had received the consideration.[142] As Dixon J later put it:

> Because value has been given on the one side, the conscience of the other party is bound when the subject comes into existence, that is, when, as is generally the case, the legal property vests in him.[143]

Put rather differently in terms but perhaps not in principle, it might be said that the assignee was charged not upon the contract itself but upon the 'equities resulting from [an] act[] done in execution of the contract'.[144]

In this way, the consequences of an abrupt change to the law would be qualified by the continuity of equitable thought and concepts. Of course, one result of the leavening effect of equitable thought and concepts upon the civil law is an apparent untidiness of general structure. This marks as doomed any attempt at neat systemization. Such a state of affairs is not a matter of regret. Equity is not to be 'stifled into homogeneity'.[145] Rather, among other things the persistence of equity helps explain the adaptation of English law, over a long period, to great economic and social changes, both in England and beyond. I would apply here the observation of Fullagar J:

> These considerations remove, or ought to remove, the temptation, which is so apt to assail us, to import a meretricious symmetry into the law.[146]

[141] cf *Napier v Hunter* [1993] AC 713 at 752.
[142] [1915] 2 Ch 345 at 360.
[143] *Palette Shoes Pty Ltd v Krohn* (1937) 58 CLR 1 at 27.
[144] *Maddison v Alderson* (1883) 8 App Cas 467 at 475.
[145] Dunn, 'Equity is Dead. Long Live Equity!' (1999) 62 *Modern Law Review* 140 at 150.
[146] *Attorney-General (NSW) v Perpetual Trustee Co. (Ltd.)* (1952) 85 CLR 237 at 285; affd (1955) 92 CLR 113; [1955] AC 457.

Lecture Three—
Federalism

It is as well to commence with the cautionary observations made in a joint judgment of four members of the High Court[1] delivered over 40 years ago. Their Honours said that:

> federalism is a form of government the nature of which is seldom adequately understood in all its bearings by those whose fortune it is to live under a unitary system. The problems of federalism and the considerations governing their solution assume a different aspect to those whose lives are spent under the operation of a federal Constitution, particularly if by education, practice and study they have been brought to think about the constitutional conceptions and modes of reasoning which belong to federalism as commonplace and familiar ideas. A unitary system presents no analogies and indeed, on the contrary, it forms a background against which many of the conceptions and distinctions inherent in federalism must strike the mind as strange and exotic refinements.[2]

The federalism of which the Court spoke was that distinctive contribution made two centuries ago to the development of democratic government in a common law system by the Constitution of the United States and, in 1867, adapted to a constitutional monarchy for Canada. In the 1890s, the framers of the Australian Constitution in some respects went beyond these models. The provisions in s 128 for

---

[1] Dixon CJ, Williams, Webb and Fullagar JJ.
[2] *O'Sullivan v Noarlunga Meat Ltd [No 2]* (1956) 94 CLR 367 at 375.

amendment by referendum submitted to the electors had
no counterpart in the Constitutions of the United States and
Canada[3]. The inspiration appears to have been found in the
Swiss Federal Constitution of 1848.[4]

De Tocqueville and, later, Bryce were two outsiders
whose appreciation of federalism in the United States went
beyond a fascination with the strange and the exotic. Dicey
was not in their league but, for a long period, even in countries such as Australia whose government was federal in
structure, it was his ideas which were imparted to genera-
tions of law students. Dicey was hostile to federalism and,
as Sir David Williams has reminded us,[5] it was Dicey who
helped give federalism a bad press in the United Kingdom
for over a century. Dicey wrote as a convinced Unionist
during the movement for Irish Home Rule led by Parnell.[6]

Dicey's lectures on the study of *The Law of the Constitution*
were published in 1885, the year before the introduction of
Gladstone's First Home Rule Bill.[7] The fourth lecture was
entitled 'Parliamentary Sovereignty and Federalism'. To
Dicey, in every true federal state there appeared 'though no
doubt with modifications' three essential characteristics.
These were the supremacy of the constitution, the distribution of the different powers of government among bodies
with limited and coordinate authority, and the authority of
the courts to act as interpreters of the constitution.[8] This

[3] Lefroy, 'The Commonwealth of Australia Bill' (1899) 15 *Law Quarterly Review* 281 at 292–3; Hogg, 'Formal Amendment of the Constitution of Canada' (Winter 1992) 55 *Law and Contemporary Problems* 253 at 254–5, 257–8.

[4] Quick and Garran, *The Annotated Constitution of the Australian Commonwealth* (1901) at 986.

[5] Williams, 'Devolution: The Welsh Perspective' in University of Cambridge Centre for Public Law, *Constitutional Reform in the United Kingdom: Practice and Principles* (1998) 41 at 46.

[6] Cosgrove, *The Rule of Law: Albert Venn Dicey, Victorian Jurist* (1980) at 114–40; Ford, *Albert Venn Dicey: The Man and His Times* (1985) at 124–46.

[7] Gladstone's Lord-Lieutenant of Ireland, Lord Carnarvon, as Colonial Secretary, had introduced in 1867 the Bill for the *British North America Act* and later favoured giving Ireland a status with the United Kingdom akin to that of a Canadian Province: Ensor, *England: 1870–1914*, (1936) at 92. See also Hadfield, *The Constitution of Northern Ireland* (1989) at 5–17; Anson, 'The Government of Ireland Bill and the Sovereignty of Parliament' (1886) 2 *Law Quarterly Review* 427.

[8] Dicey, *The Law of the Constitution* (1885) at 132, 152.

constitution must be 'written' and 'rigid'.[9] The consequences of such arrangements were said to be 'weak
government' tending to maintain the status quo and thus to
hamper schemes for wide social innovation.[10] Further:

> Federalism, lastly, means legalism—the
> predominance of the judiciary in the constitu-
> tion—the prevalence of a spirit of legality among
> the people.[11]

Dicey was writing well before the New Deal. Had he seen
that in action he might have had cause to revise his views
as to federalism bringing about 'weak government' and
hampering the institution of socially innovative schemes at
the national level. The scope offered by federalism for
diverse social development was emphasized by the
Supreme Court of Canada in its joint judgment in *Reference
re: Secession of Quebec*.[12] Federalism, the Court said, recog-
nizes the diversity of the component parts of the
Confederation, acknowledges the authority of provincial
governments to develop their societies and distributes
legislative power between the governments thought most
suited to the achievement of particular social objectives.[13]
However, there is, I suspect, still much to be said for Dicey's
last proposition that federalism means legalism.

LEGALISM

Sir Owen Dixon was of the view that close adherence to
legal reasoning was 'the only way to maintain the confidence of all parties in Federal conflicts' and that 'to judicial
decisions in great conflicts' there was no safe guide other
'than a strict and complete legalism'.[14] These remarks in
more recent times have been discounted as requiring wilful
blindness to what Holmes J called 'the felt necessities of the
time'. To the contrary, and as his decisions demonstrate, to

---

[9] Ibid., at 134.   [10] Ibid., at 157–9.   [11] Ibid., at 160.
[12] (1998) 161 DLR (4th) 385.   [13] Ibid., at 413.
[14] 'Swearing In of Sir Owen Dixon as Chief Justice' (1952) 85 CLR xi at xiv.

Dixon it was 'hardly useful to refer to the past except to
explain the present'[15] and the law should be developed not
only by 'strict logic' but also by 'high technique'.[16] Further,
the phrase 'strict and complete legalism' was uttered by a
significant equity lawyer who well appreciated that 'legalism' may include a preference of substance to form.
Nevertheless, Dixon expressed his opposition to deliberate
departures from long accepted legal principle 'in the name
of justice or of social necessity or of social convenience'; this
was going beyond seeking 'to extend the application of
accepted principles to new cases or to reason from the more
fundamental of settled legal principles to new conclusions
or to decide that a category is not closed against unforseen
instances which in reason might be subsumed thereun-
der'.[17]

That 'legalism', which is the concomitant of a federal
structure of government, is reflected in various ways, not
all of which are readily appreciated. One concerns statutory
construction. The Australian Constitution was not merely a
statute of the Imperial Parliament. The first three members
of the High Court stressed that the objective sought to be
attained by the Constitution:

> was not the establishment of a sort of municipal
> union, governed by a joint committee, like the
> union of parishes for the administration of the
> Poor Laws, say in the Isle of Wight, but the foun-
> dation of an Australian Commonwealth embrac-
> ing the whole continent with Tasmania, having a
> national character, and exercising the most ample
> powers of self-government consistent with alle-
> giance to the British Crown.[18]

Changes to the Constitution were controlled by special
provisions as to manner and form which required direct

[15]   Ibid., at xi.
[16]   Dixon, 'Concerning Judicial Method' (1956) 29 *Australian Law Journal* 468 at
471.
[17]   Ibid., at 472.
[18]   *Baxter v Commissioners of Taxation (NSW)* (1907) 4 CLR 1087 at 1108 per
Griffith CJ, Barton and O'Connor JJ.

popular participation in referenda.[19] That popular participation indicated that the source of 'sovereignty' lay outside,
or at least was not the preserve of, the Parliament. The
Constitution, like that of the United States, unavoidably
'deals in general language', it being 'not intended to
provide merely for the exigencies of a few years, but . . . to
endure through a long lapse of ages, the events of which
were locked up in the inscrutable purposes of
Providence'.[20] Further, the powers granted by the
Constitution to the federal legislature were not curtailed by
presumptions, such as compliance with public international law, which applied to statute law. To do so would be
'to apply to the establishment of legislative power a rule for
the construction of legislation passed in its exercise'.[21]

Attention is sharpened and an appreciation of distinctions in use of language fostered by the inquiries as to characterization or classification which arise on consideration
of a law made by a legislature of limited powers. The first
question is whether, 'by reference to the nature of the
rights, duties, powers and privileges which it changes,
regulates or abolishes',[22] the law is supported by an available head of power; the second is whether it trangresses
any prohibition upon the exercise of that power. For example, does a new federal law create a new species of right
and liability with respect to, say, interstate commerce? If
so, to what extent may the legislature commit to an administrative body, rather than a court, the determination of
disputed matters of fact and law respecting those new
rights and liabilities? If the new law be the law of a State,
is it invalid by reason of inconsistency with federal law?
What methods of textual or other comparison are to be
applied in the determination of inconsistency? Again, it is
too simple to speak of 'a law' in this context. Statutes may
contain a spectrum of provisions, some within, others

[19]   Constitution, s 128.
[20]   *Martin v Hunter's Lessee* 1 Wheat 304 at 326 per Story J (1816) [14 US 141 at
151] quoted in *Baxter v Commissioners of Taxation (NSW)* (1907) 4 CLR 1087 at 1105.
[21]   *Polites v The Commonwealth* (1945) 70 CLR 60 at 78 per Dixon J.
[22]   *Fairfax v Federal Commissioner of Taxation* (1965) 114 CLR 1 at 7.

beyond, legislative power. By what criterion is the good to be severed from the bad?[23]

A second aspect of 'legalism' is the analysis which federalism requires of basic precepts and principles which tend in unitary systems to be left to scholarly speculation. When 'just terms' are required to bestow validity upon a law for the compulsory acquisition of 'property', the content of the latter term assumes great practical significance. Will that which is protected in equity as 'confidential information' be classified as 'property'?[24] At what degree does legislative regulation of the enjoyment of property rights amount to a 'taking' or 'acquisition' of that property? To Viscount Simonds, the point was that no one of those rights which, in the aggregate constituted property, could by itself be called property; the denial by a Crown planning law of the right to use land in a particular way could not amount to a 'taking' of property.[25] To what degree are just terms required where the 'property' in question comprises rights and interests which are derived purely from statute and have no common law analogue?[26] If, in such a case, just terms are required, is the result to clog the freedom of one Parliament to change laws made by its predecessors?[27]

Another example concerns the doctrine of Crown immunity, which straddled the divide between substance and procedure. The operation of the Australian Constitution gives rise to species of justiciable controversy which were not encompassed by the common law as it had developed

[23] Cf *Director of Public Prosecutions v Hutchinson* [1990] 2 AC 783 at 804–9, 813, 814–19.

[24] cf *Breen v Williams* (1996) 186 CLR 71 at 81, 90.

[25] *Belfast Corporation v O D Cars Ltd* [1960] AC 490 at 517, a case upon s 5(1) of the *Government of Ireland Act* 1920 (Imp). Some reference was made by Viscount Simonds to the then state of authority in the United States and Australia. In both jurisdictions a broader view of the constitutional guarantee is now taken: Tribe, *American Constitutional Law*, 2nd edn (1988), §9.4; *Bank of NSW v The Commonwealth* (1948) 76 CLR 1 at 348–9; *Newcrest Mining (WA) Ltd v The Commonwealth* (1997) 190 CLR 513 at 531–3, 633–5.

[26] *The Commonwealth v WMC Resources Ltd* (1998) 72 ALJR 280 at 305–7, 316–17; 152 ALR 1 at 37–8, 51–3.

[27] *Kartinyeri v The Commonwealth* (1998) 72 ALJR 722 at 728–30, 736–7, 738, 741; 152 ALR 540 at 548–50, 558–60, 561–2, 566.

in England. Section 75(v) of the Constitution, long before the decision in *M v Home Office*,[28] authorized injunctive relief against officers of the Commonwealth, including Ministers of State, to restrain acts not permitted by their constitutional or legislative authority. Further, the mutual relations between the Commonwealth and States may give rise to actions between them in tort[29] and contract.[30] The result has been to recognize that, in such cases (including actions brought by individuals against the Commonwealth in contract and tort), the Constitution treats the liability as already existing, but it is 'a duty of imperfect obligation . . . made perfect by the creation of a jurisdiction in which the Crown may be sued without its consent'.[31]

Finally, the perspectives involved in the practice of federalism assist in the comprehension of the legal system as a complex whole. Within that whole are comprehended the interaction between law and equity, between judge-made law and statute, between public international and municipal law, and within the conflict of laws. This multi-planar structure is neither simple nor tidy, but nevertheless gives great strength to the legal system. From interaction at various levels comes doctrinal development. An example is the adaptation of the notion of the 'statutory fiction'[32] found in retrospective laws to the constitutional protection of the citizen whereby obedience is not required to federal and State laws which at the given moment are inconsistent. The analysis of these matters by the High Court in *University of Wollongong v Metwally*[33] was of assistance to at least some members of the House of Lords in their treatment in

[28] [1994] 1 AC 377.

[29] *The Commonwealth v New South Wales* (1923) 32 CLR 200.

[30] *South Australia v The Commonwealth* (1962) 108 CLR 130. See now *Scotland Act* 1998 (UK), s 99.

[31] *Werrin v The Commonwealth* (1938) 59 CLR 150 at 168; *The Commonwealth v Mewett* (1997) 191 CLR 471 at 491, 531, 549–52. The position in Australia and the United States is compared and contrasted in Leeming, 'The Liability of the Government under the Constitution' (1998) 17 *Australian Bar Review* 214.

[32] The term used by Windeyer J in his analysis in *Hunter Douglas Australia Pty Ltd v Perma Blinds* (1970) 122 CLR 49 at 65.

[33] (1984) 158 CLR 447.

Kleinwort Benson Ltd v Lincoln City Council[34] of the 'retrospective' effect of judicial alteration of the common law.

Further, the perspectives to which I have referred have an institutional significance. I do not know how accurate it was of Professor Stevens to say that in the United Kingdom 'there is little serious analysis of the separation of powers'.[35] However, there is much in the view that in federations where specific provision is made for the federal judicature, the result, both as a constitutional imperative[36] and as a matter of professional conduct, is to encourage judges to live solely within their co-equal branch of the constitution.

As may be apparent from the foregoing, to his analysis Dicey might well have added that with what falsely may be seen as the constriction of legalism there came a certain historicism and, thus, imprecision. It is to this that I now turn.

HISTORICISM

Professor Baker has rightly observed that lawyers have been 'bemused by the apparent continuity of their heritage into a way of thinking which inhibits historical understanding'.[37] This is apparent in the exaltation of the history of the common law, even that of criminal law and procedure,[38] as if the values of nineteenth-century liberalism were to be found in the Year Books. Improvements brought about solely by statute are overshadowed by historical mythology. The 'one golden thread' which Viscount Sankey LC said was always to be seen '[t]hroughout the web of the English Criminal Law'[39] was of fairly recent

[34] [1998] 3 WLR 1095; [1998] 4 All ER 513.

[35] Stevens, 'Judges, Politics, Politicians, and the Confusing Role of the Judiciary', in Hawkins (ed), *The Human Face of Law* (1997) 245 at 247.

[36] See *Wilson v Minister for Aboriginal and Torres Strait Islander Affairs* (1996) 189 CLR 1 at 16–18, 24–6.

[37] Baker, *The Legal Profession and the Common Law—Historical Essays* (1986) at 436.

[38] See *Pearce v The Queen* (1998) 72 ALJR 1416 at 1425; 156 ALR 684 at 696.

[39] *Woolmington v The Director of Public Prosecution* [1935] AC 462 at 481.

manufacture. The earlier portions of the Lord Chancellor's speech in *Woolmington* indicate he was aware of this development.

Professor Baker's point has particular weight with respect to constitutional historicism. This is exemplified by the recent decision of the United States Supreme Court in *Feltner v Columbia Pictures Television, Inc.*[40] The Seventh Amendment to the United States Constitution provides that:

> [i]n Suits at common law, where the value in controversy shall exceed twenty dollars, the right of trial by jury shall be preserved . . .

In 1830, the Supreme Court, in a judgment delivered by Story J, decided that the constitutional expression 'Suits at common law' referred to 'not merely suits, which the common law recognised among its old and settled proceedings, but suits in which legal rights were to be ascertained and determined, in contradistinction to those where equitable rights alone were recognised, and equitable remedies were administered'.[41] Later it was decided that the Seventh Amendment extends to 'actions brought to enforce statutory rights that are analogous to common-law causes of action ordinarily decided in English law courts in the late 18th century, as opposed to those customarily heard by courts of equity or admiralty'.[42] Here, the Supreme Court was tracing a constitutional issue as it developed in the decisions of the Court itself. History was a 'process rather than [an] event', and the Constitution was seen 'in terms of evolution and development rather than imminent meaning'.[43]

In *Feltner v Columbia Pictures Television, Inc*,[44] the Supreme

[40]   140 L Ed 2d 438 (1998).

[41]   *Parsons v Bedford* 3 Peters 433 at 447 (1830) [28 US 432 at 446] (emphasis omitted).

[42]   *Granfinanciera, SA v Nordberg* 492 US 33 at 42 (1989). See also *Curtis v Loether* 415 US 189 at 193–4 (1974).

[43]   Miller, *The Supreme Court and the Uses of History* (1969) at 191.

[44]   140 L Ed 2d 438 (1998). The Opinion of the Court was delivered by Thomas J.

Court decided that the Seventh Amendment provides a
right to jury trial on all issues pertinent to an award under
s 504(c) of the *Copyright Act* 1976. This permits a copyright
owner 'to recover, instead of actual damages and profits, an
award of statutory damages . . . in a sum of not less than
$500 or more than $20,000 as the court considers just'.[45] In
reaching that conclusion, the Supreme Court reviewed
English decisions commencing with those upon the statute
of 1710[46] as indicative of the position obtaining before the
adoption of the Seventh Amendment.[47] Here, history is
related to 'original intention'.[48] Copyright actions for
monetary recovery were tried in courts of law and thus
before juries. The authorities to which the Supreme Court
looked included the decision of the Court of King's Bench
in *Beckford v Hood*.[49] There, the jury had found a verdict for
the plaintiff in an action upon the case for damages for
infringement of the rights given to authors by the statute of
Anne, but with a reservation for the opinion of the Court *in
banc*.

Historicism also plays a significant part in the interpretation of s 96 of the Canadian *Constitution Act* 1867. This
provides for the Governor-General to appoint 'the Judges of
the Superior, District, and County Courts in each
Province'.[50] In 1996, in *Reference re Residential Tenancies Act*,[51]
the Supreme Court of Canada dealt with a challenge to the
validity of Nova Scotia legislation which provided for the
investigation, mediation, and determination of disputes
between landlords and tenants by a director of residential
tenancies and a residential tenancies board. The constitutional question was whether, in the pre-Confederation
colonies, jurisdiction over residential tenancy disputes had
been vested exclusively in courts of the kind later identified

45   The text of the provision is set out at 140 L Ed 2d 438 at 441–2 (1998).
46   8 Anne c 19.
47   66 LW 4245 at 4248 (1998).
48   See Miller, *The Supreme Court and the Uses of History* (1969) at 189–91.
49   (1798) 7 TR 620 [101 ER 1164].
50   An exception is made in respect of the courts of probate in Nova Scotia and
New Brunswick.   51   [1996] 1 SCR 186.

in s 96. The Supreme Court held that in each of the former colonies inferior courts had exercised significant concurrent jurisdiction over such disputes. It followed that it was competent for a Province to confer jurisdiction over residential tenancy matters to a tribunal appointed by the Province rather than by the Governor-General under s 96 of the Constitution.[52] The validity of the provincial legislation thus turned upon the construction of s 96. That section had been read as directing inquiry to the colonial judicial structures as they had existed before 1867.[53]

Section 90 of the Australian Constitution renders exclusive the power of the federal Parliament to impose uniform duties of customs and excise. In determining the scope of this withdrawal of 'duties of ... excise' from the States, regard has been had[54] to the use of that term in the pre-federation legislation of the colonies, to the interpretation of the power given to Congress by Art I, s 8 of the United States Constitution '[t]o lay and collect Taxes, Duties, Imposts and Excises' and to a definition which had been offered by Blackstone.[55] Again, s 49 of the Australian Constitution provides that the Senate and House of Representatives possess the powers, privileges and immunities of the House of Commons at the establishment of the Commonwealth.[56] In *R v Richards; Ex parte Fitzpatrick and Browne*,[57] Dixon CJ, in delivering the judgment of the High Court, said:

---

[52] Ibid., at 243.

[53] *Re Residential Tenancies Act, 1979* [1981] 1 SCR 714.

[54] *Ha v New South Wales* (1997) 189 CLR 465 at 493.

[55] *Commentaries on the Laws of England*, Bk 1, ch 8 at 318. Curiously, no attention appears to have been paid to Arts VII and XVIII of *The Union With Scotland Act* 1706 (6 Anne c 11). These require that 'all parts of the United Kingdom be for ever from and after the union liable to the same excises upon all exciseable liquors' (Art VII) and that the laws concerning 'such excises' be the same in Scotland from and after the union as in England (Art XVIII). See *Murray v Rogers* 1992 SLT 221 at 227.

[56] Section 49 provides that this state of affairs continues until those powers, privileges, and immunities are declared by the Parliament. Section 5 of the *Parliamentary Privileges Act* 1987 (Cth) deals with that subject but states that, except to the extent that the statute otherwise expressly provides, the operation of s 49 of the Constitution is undisturbed.

[57] (1955) 92 CLR 157; affd (1955) 92 CLR 171.

> The question, what are the powers, privileges
> and immunities of the Commons House of
> Parliament at the establishment of the
> Commonwealth, is one which the courts of law
> in England have treated as a matter for their deci-
> sion. But the courts in England arrived at that
> position after a long course of judicial decision
> not unaccompanied by political controversy. The
> law in England was finally settled about 1840.
>
> The first question is, what is that law? It must
> then be considered whether that law is, by virtue
> of the provisions which we have read, in force in
> Australia and applies to the House of
> Representatives.[58]

In all these examples, the historical 'fact' upon which the
constitutional provisions turned was ascertainable by
recourse to materials with which lawyers are accustomed to
deal. There is some relationship between the day-to-day
methodology of the judicial process and that of historical
scholarship. When a court ascertains the nature of the law
to be applied in a case through an examination of a stream
of judicial precedent, in a sense it plays the role of historian
and goes to the 'primary sources'. Greater difficulty arises
where the understanding of a constitutional provision or a
matter of constitutional structure involves an appreciation
of social, economic and political understandings at the time
of the adoption of a constitution.

In *Cole v Whitfield*,[59] the High Court referred to various
matters of history which it concluded:

> demonstrates that the principal goals of the
> movement towards the federation of the
> Australian colonies included the elimination of
> intercolonial border duties and discriminatory
> burdens and preferences in intercolonial trade
> and the achievement of intercolonial free trade.

The Court continued:

> The expression 'free trade' commonly signified

in the nineteenth century, as it does today, an absence of protectionism, ie, the protection of domestic industries against foreign competition. Such protection may be achieved by a variety of different measures—eg, tariffs that increase the price of foreign goods, non-tariff barriers such as quotas on imports, differential railway rates, subsidies on goods produced and discriminatory burdens on dealings with imports—which, alone or in combination, make importing and dealings with imports difficult or impossible.[60]

Section 92 of the Constitution had a distant ancestor in Art IV of *The Union With Scotland Act* 1706 (6 Anne c 11).[61] The Australian provision requires that 'trade, commerce, and intercourse among the States, whether by means of internal carriage or ocean navigation, shall be absolutely free'. The Court in *Cole v Whitfield* concluded that s 92 was one of several provisions designed to ensure that the Australian States 'should be a free trade area in which legislative or executive discrimination against interstate trade and commerce should be prohibited'.[62] The result was that the protectionist burdens, the imposition of which was precluded by s 92, were not only interstate border customs duties 'but also burdens, whether fiscal or non-fiscal, which discriminated against interstate trade and commerce'.[63]

The High Court has been criticized on the ground that in such passages it employs rhetorical devices to reinforce a particular archetypal view of history. In particular, it is said:

> This propensity to view history as the mere interplay of grand designs is indicated strongly when the High Court talks about the *movement*

[60] Ibid., at 392–3.

[61] Art IV requires that all the subjects of the United Kingdom of Great Britain shall have from and after the union 'full freedom and intercourse of trade and navigation to and from any port or place within the said United Kingdom and the dominions and plantations thereunto belonging'. The *Scotland Act* 1998 (UK) (s 29(2)(c) and Sched 4) denies to the Scottish Parliament the competence to modify Art IV and Art VI 'so far as they relate to freedom of trade'.

[62] (1988) 165 CLR 360 at 393.   [63] Ibid.

> *towards federation.* It is important to stress that
> this formulation is a conclusion that there was a
> movement and not an objective description of
> the data. [original emphasis][64]

This rendering of past reality into a form apt to assist as
a rhetorical device in the resolution of present conflicts is a
consequence of the application of the techniques of
common law litigation to the determination of constitutional issues. The dissatisfaction which historians may
suffer when observing the efforts of lawyers may be
compared to that suffered by philosophers when lawyers
expound 'causation'. In *March v Stramare (E & MH) Pty
Ltd*,[65] Mason CJ emphasized that the law does not accept
John Stuart Mill's definition of cause as the sum of the
conditions which are jointly sufficient to produce it and
observed:

> In philosophy and science, the concept of causa-
> tion has been developed in the context of
> explaining phenomena by reference to the rela-
> tionship between conditions and occurrences. In
> law, on the other hand, problems of causation
> arise in the context of ascertaining or apportion-
> ing legal responsibility for a given occurrence.[66]

Likewise, even where that portion of the common law
which is reproduced or reflected in constitutional text or
structure depends upon a particular view of past events,
the immediate task is to do justice between the parties in
the particular action. The determination of constitutional
issues by the procedures of common law litigation or adap-
tations thereof strengthens the notion that there is, as Lord
Wilberforce once put it, 'no higher or additional duty to
ascertain some independent truth'.[67]

[64] Schoff, 'The High Court and History: It Still Hasn't Found(ed) What It's
Looking For' (1994) 5 *Public Law Review* 253 at 258.
[65] (1991) 171 CLR 506.
[66] Ibid., at 509.
[67] *Air Canada v Secretary of State for Trade* [1983] 2 AC 394 at 438; cf Detmold,
'Original Intentions and the Race Power' (1997) 8 *Public Law Review* 244 at 246–7.

With reference to the decisions of the United States Supreme Court, it may be said that the Court has applied two rather distinct historical techniques. The first reflected the assumption that the Constitution is an instrument of static meaning and application. Professor Kelly put it as follows:

> This theory early made it important for the Court, in deciding a case, to determine the original meaning of one or another constitutional provision in order that it might be interpreted according to its aboriginal meaning, frequently couched in terms of the intent of the Constitutional Convention. The most obvious and elementary way of accomplishing this objective was a simple declaratory statement of a revelatory kind of what the original intent actually had been. As a rule this statement was allowed to stand without any supporting historical inquiry into the question at hand, an inquiry that, on occasion, might have proved distinctly embarrassing.
>
> . . . In a sense, by quoting history, the Court made history, since what it declared history to be was frequently more important than what the history might actually have been.[68]

More recently, it has been said that in the United States 'originalist appeals' offer a form of history to be employed for 'rhetorical convenience or the imperatives of law-office history'.[69] At a more basic level, 'constitutional discourse is replete with historical assertions that are at best deeply problematic and at worst, howlers'.[70] Professor Finnis has rigorously criticized the amicus briefs filed in *Webster v Reproductive Health Services*[71] and *Planned Parenthood of Southeastern Pennsylvania v Casey*[72] which set out to establish

---

[68] Kelly, 'Clio and the Court: An Illicit Love Affair', [1965] *The Supreme Court Review* 119 at 122–3.

[69] Rakove, *Original Meanings: Politics and Ideas in the Making of the Constitution* (1996) at 366.

[70] Flaherty, 'History "Lite" in Modern American Constitutionalism' (1995) 95 *Columbia Law Review* 523 at 525.   [71] 492 US 490 (1989).

[72] 505 US 833 (1992).

that, at the time of adoption of the United States Constitution, abortion was neither uncommon nor illegal. The 1989 brief was signed by a very large number of historians who are roundly condemned by Professor Finnis:

> The abandon with which it doctors, suppresses, and distorts seems to have been, if anything, enhanced by its authors' knowledge that the document was to be presented under a novel guise, as being the 'rich and accurate' work of professional historians'.[73]

But, then, one might think, history and rhetoric are no strangers and neither muse has led a cloistered life. The advocate's use of history is pragmatic and instrumental, so that if it assists to win a case it has served its purpose, whilst to the Court history is more than a mere instrument of decision. Nor, 'as the historians sometimes view it',[74] is history a research project. Rather, where it is employed in the reasoning of the Court, to which precedental force is then attached, history assists in the transmission throughout the body politic of constitutional doctrine.

The second device is the use of history as a precedent-breaking instrument, by means of which the Court returns to the original meaning and may declare that, in breaking with precedent, in truth it is maintaining constitutional continuity. *Cole v Whitfield*[75] is a recent Australian example of this technique. I have referred above to the view taken by the Court of what was involved in the movement towards federation and the free trade movement. Conclusions upon these matters were applied radically by the Court to depart from the constructions (by no means consistent *inter se*) which had been placed upon s 92 in a number of its earlier decisions given over many years.

---

[73] ' "Shameless Acts" in Colorado: Abuse of Scholarship in Constitutional Cases' [Fall 1994] *Academic Questions* 10 at 18.

[74] Miller, *The Supreme Court and the Uses of History* (1969) at 193. See also, as to the rhetorical use of history, Melton, 'Clio at the Bar: A Guide to Historical Method of Legists and Jurists', (1998) 83 *Minnesota Law Review* 377 at 424–34.

[75] (1988) 165 CLR 360.

The first use of historical method is still very much with us, particularly in the United States, but also elsewhere, in the debate as to the significance of 'original intent'. On that subject there is a vast and increasing literature. One might wonder why this is so in societies which, as presently constituted, are not known readily to defer to past wisdom. Further, do we, as Professor Rakove (who writes as an historian) puts it,[76] 'truly believe that language can only mean now what it meant then'?

In Australia, the constitutional text itself[77] indicates that what thereafter was to be regarded as 'the Constitution' was to be the text as expounded by courts exercising the judicial power of the Commonwealth. Moreover, those who framed the Constitution a century ago were doing more than simply collecting and hoarding conventional doctrines and usages drawn from the United Kingdom and from the federal systems of the United States and Canada at the stage to which they had then developed. For example, it is now settled that the text and structure of the Constitution gives effect to a system of representative and responsible government.[78] However, it was necessary to adapt doctrinal principle of representative government to federalism. The framers approached their task in such a way as to allow room for further legislative evolution in the system of representative government, particularly with respect to the franchise. By this means they avoided, to a significant degree, constitutional rigidity.[79]

The framers of the Australian Constitution were well aware of what lay ahead. One of them, Alfred Deakin,[80] speaking in 1902 as Attorney-General upon the Bill for what is now the *Judiciary Act* 1903 (Cth), made the point that it was unlikely that it would be a difficult task to alter the Constitution by the mechanism provided in s 128, and continued:

---

[76] *Original Meanings: Politics and Ideas in the Making of the Constitution* (1996) at 368. [77] s 74, s 76(ii).

[78] *Lange v Australian Broadcasting Corporation* (1997) 189 CLR 520 at 557.

[79] *McGinty v Western Australia* (1996) 186 CLR 140 at 269.

[80] 1856–1919. First Attorney-General and second Prime Minister of Australia.

In the meantime, the statute stands and will
stand on the statute-book just as in the hour in
which it was assented to. But the nation lives,
grows, and expands. Its circumstances change,
its needs alter, and its problems present themselves with new faces. The organ of the national
life which preserving the union is yet able from
time to time to transfuse into it the fresh blood of
the living present, is the Judiciary the High Court
of Australia or Supreme Court in the United
States. It is as one of the organs of Government
which enables the Constitution to grow and to be
adapted to the changeful necessities and circumstances of generation after generation that the
High Court operates. Amendments achieve
direct and sweeping changes, but the court
moves by gradual, often indirect, cautious, well
considered steps, that enable the past to join the
future, without undue collision and strife in the
present.[81]

FEDERALISM, THE COMMON LAW AND PARLIAMENTARY SUPREMACY

This relationship is of abiding interest and concern, perhaps
particularly now in the United Kingdom. The subject is one
with which the High Court recently was required to deal in
Lange v Australian Broadcasting Corporation.[82] It was necessary
there to consider the relationship between the Australian
Constitution and the freedom of communication which it
requires on the one hand and the common law and the
statute law which govern the law of defamation on the other.

In an address given in the United States in 1943, Sir Owen
Dixon said:

We do not of course treat the common law as a
transcendental body of legal doctrine, but we do

[81] Commonwealth, House of Representatives, *Parliamentary Debates*
(Hansard), 18 March 1902, vol 8 at 10967–8.
[82] (1997) 189 CLR 520. See also *Reynolds v Times Newspapers Ltd* [1998] 3 All ER
961 at 989–90, 1002–3.

treat it as antecedent in operation to the constitutional instruments which first divided Australia
into separate Colonies and then united her in a
federal Commonwealth. We therefore regard
Australian law as a unit. Its content comprises
besides legislation the general common law
which it is the duty of the courts to ascertain as
best they may. . . . The anterior operation of the
common law in Australia is not just a dogma of
our legal system, an abstraction of our constitutional reasoning. It is a fact of legal history.[83]

It was against that background that in *Lange* the Court
approached its task as follows:[84]

It is appropriate to begin with the Parliament
at Westminster. To say of the United Kingdom
that it has an 'unwritten constitution' is to identify an amalgam of common law and statute and
to contrast it with a written constitution which is
rigid rather than fluid. The common law supplies
elements of the British constitutional fabric.
Sir Owen Dixon wrote:[85] 'The British conception
of the complete supremacy of Parliament developed under the common law; it forms part of the
common law and, indeed, it may be considered
as deriving its authority from the common law
rather than as giving authority to the common
law. But, after all, the common law was the
common law of England. It was not a law of
nations. It developed no general doctrine that all
legislatures by their very nature were supreme
over the law.'

With the establishment of the Commonwealth
of Australia, as with that of the United States of
America, it became necessary to accommodate

---

[83] 'Sources of Legal Authority', reprinted in *Jesting Pilate*, (1965) 198 at 199 and
in (1943) 17 *Australian Law Journal* 138 at 139. See also *Cheatle v The Queen* (1993)
177 CLR 541 at 552; *Theophanous v Herald & Weekly Times Ltd* (1994) 182 CLR 104 at
141–2.

[84] (1997) 189 CLR 520 at 562–3.

[85] 'Sources of Legal Authority', reprinted in *Jesting Pilate* (1965) 198 at 199–200
and in (1943) 17 *Australian Law Journal* 138 at 139.

basic common law concepts and techniques to a
federal system of government embodied in a
written and rigid constitution. The outcome in
Australia differs from that in the United States.
There is but one common law in Australia which
is declared by this Court as the final court of
appeal. In contrast to the position in the United
States, the common law as it exists throughout
the Australian States and Territories is not frag-
mented into different systems of jurisprudence,
possessing different content and subject to different authoritative interpretations.[86]

Restraints upon the exercise of legislative power, without
more, impose but an imperfect obligation. The obligation is
imperfect by reason both of the capacity of the legislature
later to remove the restraint and of the absence of a judicial
power to enforce compliance with the obligation. The first
notion is perhaps best expressed by speaking of the distinction between a rigid and a fluid constitution and the latter
by invoking 'justiciability' at the expense of 'parliamentary
supremacy'.

The first, a rigid constitution, may be present without the
second but requires it for an effective operation. The point
may be illustrated by the decisions from Scotland upon *The
Union With Scotland Act* 1706[87] or, more accurately, upon the
Scottish statute, *Act Ratifying and Approving the Treaty of
Union of the Kingdoms of Scotland and England* 1707.[88] The
Articles to which I have referred earlier in this lecture are so
expressed as to suggest restraints upon the power of the
new Parliament of Great Britain established by Art III. For
example, the concluding sentence of Art XVIII stipulates
'that no alteration be made in laws which concern private

---

[86]　Cf *Black & White Taxi Co v Brown & Yellow Taxi Co* 276 US 518 at 533–4 (1928);
Erie Railroad Co v Tompkins 304 US 64 at 78–9 (1938).

[87]　6 Anne c 11.

[88]　Act 1707 c 7. I am not unmindful of what, in his British Academy Lecture,
Professor MacCormick identified as 'the ideological resonance attaching to the
rival phraseologies "the Act of Union", "the Acts of Union", "the Articles of
Union" and "the treaty of Union" ': 'The English Constitution, the British State,
and the Scottish Assembly', (1997).

right except for evident utility of the subjects within Scotland'.

To Sir Owen Dixon, whilst little attention appeared to have been given to the basis of the authority of the Parliament established by the Union of the Kingdoms, 'it cannot be considered anything but a new Parliament'.[89] It was 'endowed with constituent as well as ordinary legislative power'.[90] The next question was '[h]ow then can it be said that the supremacy of the Parliament of the United Kingdom is part of the common law?'[91] This was done by accepting the new Parliament as having the supremacy over the law which belonged to the English Parliament so that '[t]he plentitude of its authority was measured by the doctrine of the common law'.[92]

There is a further question, much considered[93] at the time of *Harris v Minister of the Interior*,[94] as to whether the fundamentals of sovereignty are attacked by provisions which purport to bind the successors of a Parliament in a unitary system with respect to the manner and form required for certain legislative amendments or repeals. Is not the doctrine 'part of the metaphysics of the conception of sovereignty?'[95] If the doctrine of Parliamentary supremacy be but part of the common law, may it not be altered by the legislature?

The decisions in Scotland have tended to treat the provisions of the Union of 1707 as 'fundamental law', or to allow of that possibility but accept that the courts lack authority to entertain an issue as to whether the fundamental law has

---

[89] Dixon, 'The Common Law as an Ultimate Constitutional Foundation' (1957) 31 *Australian Law Journal* 240 at 243.

[90] Cf *Clayton v Heffron* (1960) 105 CLR 214 at 251.

[91] Dixon, 'The Common Law as an Ultimate Constitutional Foundation' (1957) 31 *Australian Law Journal* 240 at 243.

[92] Ibid.

[93] Wade, 'The Basis of Legal Sovereignty' [1955] *Cambridge Law Journal* 172 at 177 ff; Cowen, 'Parliamentary Sovereignty and the Limits of Legal Change' (1952) 26 *Australian Law Journal* 237 at 239.

[94] [1952] 2 SA 428.

[95] Dixon, 'The Common Law as an Ultimate Constitutional Foundation' (1957) 31 *Australian Law Journal* 240 at 242.

been broken by the Parliament.[96] It recently has been well put that 'justiciability and constitutional illegality are separate concepts'.[97]

In part, as Lord Kirkwood observed,[98] with reference to *R v Secretary of State for Transport, Ex parte Factortame Ltd,*[99] this doctrine of parliamentary supremacy has rested upon the absence of machinery (in particular, of power to enjoin the Crown by interim injunction) whereby the validity of a statute could be brought under review by the courts. This may be compared with the position in a federation such as Australia, where the High Court has treated as justiciable the question whether a statute had been 'duly passed' by the federal legislature under special provisions of the Constitution dealing with the joint sitting of both chambers.[100]

With respect to interim relief where validity of a law is in issue, the *American Cyanamid*[101] doctrine applies in Australia only in a severely modified form. As in Canada,[102] the principle is that '[i]n the absence of compelling grounds, it is the duty of the Court to respect, indeed, to defer to, the enactment of the legislature until that enactment is adjudged ultra vires'.[103]

The immediate effect of the holding of the European Court of Justice ('the ECJ') in *Factortame* with respect to interim relief was that, in a protection of rights under Community law, national courts were not to be inhibited by rules of national law from granting interim relief, leaving it to national courts to determine whether an appropriate case

[96] *MacCormick v Lord Advocate* 1953 SC 396 at 412–13; *Gibson v Lord Advocate* 1975 SLT 134 at 137; *Pringle, Petitioner* 1991 SLT 330 at 333; *Murray v Rogers* 1992 SLT 221 at 225, 227–8.

[97] Addo and Smith, 'The Relevance of Historical Fact to Certain Arguments Relating to the Legal Significance of the Acts of Union' [1998] *Juridical Review* 37 at 60.   [98] *Murray v Rogers* 1992 SLT 221 at 228.

[99] [1990] 2 AC 85 at 150.

[100] *Western Australia v The Commonwealth* (1975) 134 CLR 201; cf *Western Australia v The Commonwealth (Native Title Act Case)* (1995) 183 CLR 373 at 482.

[101] *American Cyanamid Co v Ethicon Ltd* [1975] AC 396.

[102] *Morgentaler v Ackroyd* (1983) 42 OR (2d) 659 at 668.

[103] *Castlemaine Tooheys Ltd v South Australia* (1986) 161 CLR 148 at 155–6 per Mason ACJ.

for the grant of interim relief was made out.[104] In working out that rule, the guidelines laid down in *American Cyanamid*[105] were influential. The House of Lords eschewed any rule that a party challenging the validity of a law must show a strong prima facie case that the law was invalid[106]. Counsel had not invited attention to those decisions from Commonwealth federations to which I have referred and which might have indicated a different approach.

THE EUROPEAN UNION

In *Murray v Rogers*,[107] Lord Hope indicated that a different situation to that with respect to the Union of 1707 obtained where a statute was said to be 'incompatible with Community law'; this was because the possibility of a measure being held invalid by a competent court was 'embodied in Community law itself'.

Speaking with respect to the interim relief sought and ultimately obtained in the *Factortame* litigation,[108] Lord Neill of Bladon has said:

> [T]he English courts, after an initial display of reluctance, were finally driven to accept the full rigour of Community law in the embarrassing litigation concerning the Common Fisheries Policy and the Spanish trawlers. Compliance with Community law, as expounded by the ECJ, obliged the House of Lords, where there was a serious doubt as to the validity of UK legislation, to take the unprecedented step of granting an injunction against the Crown and putting UK legislation into suspense pending a final ruling by the ECJ.[109]

---

[104]   *R v Secretary of State for Transport, Ex parte Factortame Ltd (No 2)* [1991] 1 AC 603 at 659.   [105]   *American Cyanamid Co v Ethicon Ltd* [1975] AC 396.

[106]   [1991] 1 AC 603 at 674.   [107]   1992 SLT 221 at 225.

[108]   *R v Secretary of State for Transport, Ex parte Factortame Ltd* [1990] 2 AC 85; *R v Secretary of State for Transport, Ex parte Factortame Ltd (No 2)* [1991] 1 AC 603. The next stage is the decision of the European Court of Justice in *Brasserie du Pêcheur SA v Federal Republic of Germany [Factortame No 4]* [1996] QB 404.

[109]   Lord Neill, 'The European Court of Justice: A Case Study in Judicial Activism', *European Policy Forum*, August 1995 at 11 (footnote omitted).

How has this come to pass by a means short of entrenchment of Community law as the benchmark by reference to
which the validity of the laws made by the United
Kingdom Parliament is to be measured? Is there now an
operative federal structure of which that Parliament and
the British courts are an element? After all, as Sir Owen
Dixon once pointed out,[110] one 'general principle' of federalism concerns the means by which effect is given to the
supremacy of one body of law over another and the result
in any given case is 'a typical product of federalism'.[111]

The answer appears to lie, at least on the surface, not in
the acceptance of any federal law-making structure nor in
the adoption of the doctrine in *Marbury v Madison*.[112]
Rather, the *European Communities Act 1972* ('the 1972 Act')
in s 2(1) 'picks up' 'rights, powers, liabilities, obligations
and restrictions' which are 'from time to time created or
arising by or under' the European Economic Community
Treaty laws (broadly defined in s 1(2) as 'the Treaties').
Section 2(4) requires by its own force other British laws to
be 'construed and have effect' accordingly.

Further, the Treaties which are lifted into British law in
this way confer upon the ECJ a final power of judicial
review to determine inconsistency or incompatibility.
Article 164 of the Treaty of Rome states:

> The [ECJ] shall ensure that in the interpretation
> and application of this Treaty the law is
> observed.

Article 177 deals with the relationship with what have come
to be called national courts and the ECJ. At the time of the
Factortame litigation, it provided:

> The [ECJ] shall have jurisdiction to give prelimi-
> nary rulings concerning:
>
> (*a*) the interpretation of this Treaty;
>
> (*b*) the validity and interpretation of Acts of the
> institutions of the Community;

---

110 *O'Sullivan v Noarlunga Meat Ltd [No 2]* (1956) 94 CLR 367 at 374.
111 Ibid., at 376.   112 1 Cranch 137 (1803) [5 US 87].

(*c*) the interpretation of the statutes and bodies
established by an Act of the Council, where those
statutes so provide.

Where such a question is raised before a court or
tribunal of a Member State, that court or tribunal
may, if it considers that a decision on the question is necessary to enable it to give judgment,
request the [ECJ] to give a ruling thereon.

Where any such question is raised in a case pending before a court or tribunal of a Member State
against whose decisions there is no judicial
remedy under the national law, that court or
tribunal shall bring the matter before the [ECJ].

To one whose life is spent under the operation of a federal
Constitution to which the common law is antecedent, in the
sense identified by Sir Owen Dixon, several questions arise.
The first concerns interpretation. It has been said in an
English court:

The interpretation of Community instruments
involves very often not the process familiar to
common lawyers of laboriously extracting the
meaning from words used but the more creative
process of supplying flesh to a spare and loosely
constructed skeleton.[113]

At the level of construction of legislation, rather than the
determination of its validity, this situation now occurs
fairly frequently in common law jurisdictions. This is a by-
product of the legislative practice of directly enacting into
municipal law what might be thought loosely or impre-
cisely drawn international obligations. Refugee law is a
striking example. Municipal courts may be drawn into the
application of the general rule of interpretation provided
by Art 31 of the Vienna Convention on the Law of
Treaties.[114] At the level of constitutional interpretation,
judges trained in the common law tradition have, for a

---

[113] *Customs and Excise Commissioners v ApS Samex* [1983] 1 All ER 1042 at 1056.
[114] *Applicant A v Minister for Immigration and Ethnic Affairs* (1997) 190 CLR 225
at 251–6; cf *T v Home Secretary* [1996] AC 742 at 766–8.

lengthy period, been engaged in the creative process of
supplying flesh to a spare and loosely constructed skeleton
of fundamental law.

The classic text was supplied by Marshall CJ in *McCulloch
v Maryland*,[115] decided by the Supreme Court of the United
States at the 1819 term. The Court upheld the power of
Congress to incorporate the Second Bank of the United
States while denying the right of a state to tax the bank. The
primary canon of constitutional interpretation expounded
by Marshall CJ recently has been summarized as follows:

> The framers, Marshall observed, deliberately
> eschewed writing a Constitution that partook 'of
> the prolixity of a legal code'. They intended to
> mark only the 'great outlines', to designate the
> 'important objects', leaving the multiplicity of
> subordinate governmental powers involved in
> those objects to 'be deduced from the nature of
> the objects themselves'. Therefore, said Marshall
> in a memorable phrase, in conducting an inquiry
> into the extent and scope of the delegated
> powers, 'we must never forget that it is *a consti-
> tution* we are expounding'. [original empha-
> sis][116]

That phrase is echoed in decisions given in other federal
jurisdictions.[117]

The second matter concerns the criteria by which it will
be determined whether 'rights, powers, liabilities, obligations and restrictions' truly 'aris[e] by or under' the Treaties
within the meaning of s 2(1). In the United States
Constitution,[118] the federal judicial power extends to all
cases 'arising under' the Constitution, the laws of the

---

[115] 4 Wheat 316 (1819) [17 US 159].

[116] Hobson, *The Great Chief Justice: John Marshall and the Rule of Law* (1996) at
119.

[117] For example, *Polites v The Commonwealth* (1945) 70 CLR 60 at 78; *R v Public
Vehicles Licensing Appeal Tribunal (Tas); Ex parte Australian National Airways Pty Ltd*
(1964) 113 CLR 207 at 225–6; *Owners of 'Shin Kobe Maru' v Empire Shipping Co Inc*
(1994) 181 CLR 404 at 424; *Re Dingjan; Ex parte Wagner* (1995) 183 CLR 323 at 352–3,
368; *Leask v The Commonwealth* (1996) 187 CLR 579 at 621.

[118] Art III, s 2.

CHANGE AND CONTENTS   1   25.00
NEW RUSSIAN FOREIG   1   11.51
                   TOTAL   36.51

CARD NUMBER   3742831624x2912
START DATE   0699
EXPIRY DATE   0301
MERCHANT ID   9423509413
AUTHORISATION CODE   00000035
AMERICAN EXPRESS   SALE   36.51

                           10/10/99 13:17

United States, and treaties. In Australia, the federal jurisdiction includes matters '[a]rising under' the Constitution, or involving its interpretation, and matters '[a]rising under' any federal laws.[119]

There is an extensive body of authority construing the phrase 'arising under' in this context. In Art III, s 2 of the United States Constitution, the phrase includes both situations where there is a cause of action created by federal law and instances where the case might turn on a question of federal law even if it not be an actual basis for the decision.[120] In Australia, a matter arises under a federal law if the right or duty in question in the matter owes its existence to federal law or depends upon federal law for its enforcement. This is so whether or not the determination of the controversy involves the interpretation, or validity, of the law. Likewise, a matter arises under federal law if the source of a defence which asserts that the defendant is immune from the liability or obligation alleged against that party is a federal law.[121]

The next matter concerns the identification of the criteria for determination of that inconsistency or incompatibility which flows from construing other British laws as having effect according to the Treaties, within the meaning of s 2(4) of the 1972 Act. The term 'incompatible' is used by the House of Lords to identify the relationship between national law and European law and in framing declaratory relief.[122] The notions involved here have a long history in what once was the law of the British Empire. Section 2 of

[119] Constitution, s 76(i), (ii).

[120] *City of Chicago v International College of Surgeons* 139 L Ed 2d 525 at 534–6 (1997); Chemerinsky, *Federal Jurisdiction*, 2nd edn (1994), §5.2.2; Oakley, 'Federal Jurisdiction and the Problem of the Litigative Unit: When Does What "Arise Under" Federal Law' (1998) 76 *Texas Law Review* 1829.

[121] *LNC Industries Ltd v BMW (Australia) Ltd* (1983) 151 CLR 575 at 581; *Re McJannet; Ex parte Australian Workers' Union of Employees (Q) [No 2]* (1997) 189 CLR 654 at 656–7.

[122] See *R v Secretary of State for Employment, Ex parte Equal Opportunities Commission* [1995] 1 AC 1 at 31–2. In *Garland v British Rail Engineering Ltd* [1983] 2, AC 751 at 771, Lord Diplock used the term 'inconsistent'. As Diplock KC, he had appeared in the same interest as Sir Garfield Barwick in *Commonwealth of Australia v Bank of New South Wales* [1950] AC 235 at 261.

the *Colonial Laws Validity Act* 1865 (Imp)[123] spoke of the
'repugnancy' between Imperial and colonial laws.[124] The
term 'repugnant' was used interchangeably with 'contrari-
ety' in commissions to Governors and in Colonial Charters
from the earliest times of English colonization.[125]

The term 'inconsistent' (and this must be true of 'incompatible') is one whose meaning is by no means self-evident
when applied to a relationship between two laws. There is
a range of possible meanings.[126] Many of these have been
adopted in the constitutional law of Australia and other
federations with respect to conflict between federal and
State or Provincial laws made in exercise of concurrent
legislative powers.

It may be impossible to obey both laws because one
prohibits under penalty that which the other requires. An
example is a State law which authorizes and commands a
vote on a day on which a federal law authorizes and
commands a federal election and the federal law forbids
any other vote on the same day.[127] Alternatively, one law
may merely alter, impair or detract from the operation of
the other law, with simultaneous obedience being possible,
but nevertheless there may be inconsistency in the constitutional sense.[128] The conduct of a particular business may
require compliance with federal and State regulatory
regimes. Thus, a commercial broadcaster may require a
licence under federal media law and approval under State
environmental law.[129] Again, it may appear from the terms,
nature or the subject-matter of one law that it was intended

[123] 28 & 29 Vict c 63.

[124] See *Attorney-General for Queensland v Attorney-General for the Commonwealth*
(1915) 20 CLR 148 at 167–8; *Union Steamship Co of New Zealand Ltd v The
Commonwealth* (1925) 36 CLR 130 at 148–50, 156–9; *University of Wollongong v
Metwally* (1984) 158 CLR 447 at 464.

[125] *Attorney-General for Queensland v Attorney-General for the Commonwealth*
(1915) 20 CLR 148 at 168.

[126] Tammelo, 'The Test of Inconsistency Between Commonwealth and State
Laws' (1957) 30 *Australian Law Journal* 496.

[127] *R v Brisbane Licensing Court; Ex parte Daniell* (1920) 28 CLR 23 at 29.

[128] *Ex parte McLean* (1930) 43 CLR 472 at 483; *Victoria v The Commonwealth*
(1937) 58 CLR 618 at 630.

[129] *Commercial Radio Coffs Harbour v Fuller* (1986) 161 CLR 47 at 58–9.

as a complete statement of the law governing a particular subject-matter or set of rights and duties with which the other law purports to deal. In such cases the latter law, if made by a subordinate legislature, must yield as inconsistent with the former law.[130] This is the doctrine concerned with the covering or pre-emption of the field by federal law, to which I made brief reference in the first of these lectures.[131]

Where the laws in question are those of the one legislature, there is a presumption that the legislature intended both statutes to operate.[132] However, its very terms show that is not the case with respect to s 2 of the 1972 Act. Some analogy may be drawn with The Canadian Bill of Rights as first enacted in 1960, that is to say, without constitutional entrenchment. Section 2 thereof stated that every law of Canada was, unless expressly declared by statute, to operate notwithstanding the Bill of Rights, to be so construed and applied as not to prejudice the enumerated rights and freedoms.[133] However, perhaps the most striking feature of s 2 of the 1972 Act is that it deals not with laws of the one legislature which are concurrently in operation but rather 'picks up' and gives paramountcy to laws emanating from another, non-domestic, law-making institution. Hence, one would think, what is involved is a typical product of federalism which invites further analysis.

Is this system of paramountcy 'self-executing'? The meaning of that term may be seen from decisions construing the inconsistency provision (s 109) of the Australian Constitution. The federal and State laws may confer but a concurrent or parallel power upon either or both of the respective executive branches in relation to the same subject

---

[130] *Victoria v The Commonwealth* (1937) 58 CLR 618 at 630; cf *Union Steamship Co of Australia Pty Ltd v King* (1988) 166 CLR 1 at 14–16.

[131] See 'The Common Law and Statute', especially text accompanying fnn 138 and 139.

[132] *Project Blue Sky Inc v Australian Broadcasting Authority* (1998) 72 ALJR 841 at 855–6; 153 ALR 490 at 509–10.

[133] See *R v Drybones* [1970] SCR 282. A somewhat similar legislative scheme was adopted with ss 4–8 of the *New Zealand Bill of Rights Act* 1990 (NZ).

(for example, to compel the removal of shipwrecks).[134] Where such a power has been conferred by the federal law, inconsistency arises only when the Minister imposes on the shipowner an obligation. The issue then is whether the federal law implies that, in discharging that obligation, the shipowner is to act without interference by any other public authority.[135] However, for so long as inconsistency does exist, s 109 of its own force deprives the State law of validity. The Constitution thus protects the individual from competing demands made by inconsistent laws. It does so by conferring a constitutional right to ignore the State law.[136]

In *Factortame*,[137] the appellants urged upon the House of Lords that their 'individual rights' had 'existed in law *ab initio*' and were entitled to protection on an interim basis. The Solicitor-General put the opposite view, contending:

> There is nothing in the Act of 1972 that requires or entitles British courts to suspend an Act of Parliament. Section 2(4), which provides that any enactment, whether passed before or after the Act of 1972, shall be construed and have effect subject to directly applicable Community law rights, enables the courts to reconcile conflicts between Community law and domestic provisions and enactments. It can have no application until the extent of the directly applicable Community law rights are determined, thus establishing definitively the 'enforceable Community right' to be given effect in accordance with section 2(1) of the Act. This interpretation of the Act is consistent with the approach of Lord Denning MR in *Macarthys Ltd v Smith*.[138] Section 2(1) means that, when the scope of directly applicable Community law rights is

---

[134] *Victoria v The Commonwealth* (1937) 58 CLR 618.

[135] Ibid., at 631.

[136] *University of Wollongong v Metwally* (1984) 158 CLR 447 at 457–8, 476–7; *Croome v Tasmania* (1997) 190 CLR 119 at 129–30.

[137] [1990] 2 AC 85 at 100.

[138] [1981] QB 180 at 200.

definitively established, immediate and retrospective effect must be given to those rights.
Section 2(4) gives effect to the United Kingdom's
treaty obligation to secure the primacy of directly
applicable Community law. It follows that, if it
were established that the application of primary
legislation passed after the Act of 1972 would be
inconsistent with directly applicable Community
law rights, the courts would have jurisdiction to
grant appropriate relief in judicial review
proceedings giving effect to those rights. That
could include relief the effect of which would be
to disapply pro tanto express provisions of a
statute found to be incompatible with
Community law.[139]

It is far from my purpose to canvass which view was
correct. What is significant is that, presumably by reason of
s 2 of the 1972 Act, the House regarded itself as obliged by
Art 177 of the Treaty to seek a ruling from the ECJ, which
answered that:

Community law must be interpreted as meaning
that a national court which, in a case before it
concerning Community law, considers that the
sole obstacle which precludes it from granting
interim relief is a rule of national law must set
aside that rule.[140]

Well before the accession of the United Kingdom to the
Treaty of Rome, the ECJ had declared in *Flaminio Costa v
ENEL (National Electricity Board)*[141] that, in contrast with
ordinary international treaties, 'the EEC Treaty has created
its own legal system which, on the entry into force of the
Treaty, became an integral part of the legal systems of the
Member States and which their courts are bound to apply'
and continued:

By creating a Community of unlimited duration,
having its own institutions, its own personality,

[139] Ibid., at 114.
[140] *R v Secretary of State for Transport, Ex parte Factortame Ltd (No 2)* [1991] 1 AC
603 at 644–5.   [141] [1964] ECR 585 at 593.

its own legal capacity and capacity of representa-
tion on the international plane and, more particularly, real powers stemming from a limitation of
sovereignty or a transfer of powers from the
States to the Community, the Member States
have limited their sovereign rights, albeit within
limited fields, and have thus created a body of
law which binds their nationals and themselves.

That is reminiscent of the language of the 'Federal
Compact' and would, one might think, readily have been
understood by Marshall CJ. The conundrum is that if, on
one level, the result in *Factortame* involves no more than the
operation of s 2 of the 1972 Act, that provision, although not
expressed in the language of constitutional entrenchment,
has adopted a legal order which appears to differ in nature
and kind from that which produced s 2 itself.

The point is highlighted by the remarks of Hoffmann J in
Stoke-on-Trent City Council v B & Q Plc:

> The EEC Treaty is the supreme law of this coun-
> try, taking precedence over Acts of Parliament.
> Our entry into the European Economic
> Community meant that (subject to our undoubted
> but probably theoretical right to withdraw from
> the Community altogether) Parliament surren-
> dered its sovereign right to legislate contrary to
> the provisions of the Treaty on the matters of
> social and economic policy which it regulated.[142]

The views of Sir Owen Dixon concerning the relationship
between the doctrine of parliamentary supremacy, the
common law and statute[143] return to mind. The statute
involved in the *Factortame* litigation was the *Merchant
Shipping Act* 1988 (UK). Where was the mechanism which
entrenched s 2 of the 1972 Act? One answer, deplored by
Professor Sir William Wade,[144] is to 'turn a blind eye to
constitutional theory altogether'.

---

[142] [1991] Ch 48 at 56.   [143] See text accompanying fnn 83–5.
[144] 'Sovereignty—Revolution or Evolution?' (1996) 112 *Law Quarterly Review*
568 at 575.

One is left with the impression that, although still not fully in sight, the grundnorm has moved. That impression is greatly strengthened by the formulation by the ECJ in *Factortame No 4*[145] of the 'principle' by which a member state is obliged to make good damage caused to individuals by breach of Community law attributable to that state. As a sequel, the Queen's Bench Divisional Court declared that, whilst the breaches did not found any claim to exemplary damages, they 'were sufficiently serious to give rise to liability for any damage that may subsequently be shown to have been caused to the applicants'.[146] The result may be compared with that considered under the heading 'Legalism' with respect to Crown immunity in a federation with a common law system.[147]

DEVOLUTION IN SCOTLAND

The 'legislative competence' of the Scottish Parliament bestowed by the *Scotland Act* 1998 (UK) is limited by s 29. Legislation is to be read, as far as possible, so as to be within that competence (s 101). Sub-sections (1) and (2) of s 29 are in these terms:

> (1) An Act of the Scottish Parliament is not law so far as any provision of the Act is outside the legislative competence of the Parliament.
>
> (2) A provision is outside that competence so far as any of the following paragraphs apply—
>
> > (a) it would form part of the law of a country or territory other than Scotland, or confer or remove functions exercisable otherwise than in or as regards Scotland,

---

[145] *Brasserie du Pêcheur SA v Federal Public of Germany* [1996] QB 404 at 506. See Deards, ' "Curiouser and Curiouser"? The Development of Member State Liability in the Court of Justice' (1997) 3 *European Public Law* 117 at 120–6; Lewis, 'Damages and the Right to an Effective Remedy for Breach of European Community Law' in Forsyth and Hare (eds), *The Golden Metwand and the Crooked Cord*, (1998) 319 at 322–4.

[146] *R v Secretary of State for Transport, Ex parte Factortame Ltd* [1998] 1 All ER 736 (Note). [147] See text accompanying fnn 28–31.

(*b*) it relates to reserved matters,

(*c*) it is in breach of the restrictions in Schedule 4,

(*d*) it is incompatible with any of the Convention rights or with Community law,

(*e*) it would remove the Lord Advocate from his position as head of the systems of criminal prosecution and investigation of deaths in Scotland.

However, s 99(1) provides that rights and liabilities may arise between the Crown in right of the United Kingdom and in right of Scotland 'by virtue of a contract, by operation of law or by virtue of an enactment as they may arise between subjects'. It would seem from s 99(3) that the Crown in one right may sue the Crown in the other right in respect of those matters. This state of affairs displays what often is seen as a characteristic of 'federal jurisdiction' where doctrines of Crown immunity are displaced.[148]

The absence of any entrenchment provision with respect to the structure to be established by the *Scotland Act* is a significant matter. With limited exceptions, the provisions of the *Scotland Act* may not be modified by the Scottish Parliament.[149] However, there is no restraint upon the Parliament at Westminster doing so.[150] Further, the schedule of 'reserved matters'[151] may be modified under s 30(2) by Order in Council as considered 'necessary or expedient' by the Executive Government of the United Kingdom. Presumably, the expansion of the list of reserved matters may thereupon but not with retroactive effect place a pre-existing law of the Scottish Parliament outside its legislative competence.

The result is to deny that attribute of federalism which fixes upon constitutional arrangements which are both

---

[148] *The Commonwealth v Mewett* (1997) 191 CLR 471.

[149] s 29(2)(c); Sched 4, cl 4.   [150] s 28(7).

[151] Sched 5. This includes such subjects as registration and funding of political parties, foreign affairs, the Civil Service, and defence.

written and rigid. Hence the force of the observation that in respect of Scotland there will be a delegation rather than a division of legislative powers. The legislative competence of the Scottish Parliament may change pursuant to Orders in Council made under the power in s 30(2). Further, there is no fixed requirement of manner and form, such as that which attends changes to divisions of legislative powers in federal systems, for the recall of the *Scotland Act* by further legislation from Westminster.

The entrenchment of the structure now established for Scotland (the outline of which has popular validation by referendum) may be thought likely to be political rather than legal in character. The Scottish Parliament may prove to be permanent because no future Parliament at Westminster may have sufficient will to abolish it.[152] An Australian analogy may help make the point. Section 122 of the Australian Constitution confers upon the Parliament of the Commonwealth power to make laws 'for the government of' the Australian Capital Territory and the Northern Territory. Such laws have in each case conferred a measure of 'self-government' which included the establishment of a Territorial legislature.[153] Nevertheless, the Parliament of the Commonwealth on occasion thereafter has exercised its legislative power under s 122 with respect to what might be thought 'domestic' matters of a Territory.[154] However, in general, political pressures, both at the Territorial and federal levels, militate against such intervention.

Notwithstanding the foregoing, questions may be expected to arise with respect to the powers *inter se* of the legislative and executive branches of government at

---

[152] Brazier, 'The Scotland Bill as Constitutional Legislation' (1998) 19 *Statute Law Review* 12 at 14.

[153] *Northern Territory (Self-Government) Act* 1978 (Cth); *Australian Capital Territory (Self-Government) Act* 1988 (Cth).

[154] The *Euthanasia Laws Act* 1997 (Cth) limited the legislative power previously conferred on the Northern Territory, Australian Capital Territory and Norfolk Island Legislative Assemblies so as to exclude the making of laws which permitted euthanasia and, in the case of the Northern Territory, expressly provided that an enactment of its Legislative Assembly, the *Rights of the Terminally Ill Act* 1995 (NT), had no force or effect as a law of that Territory.

Edinburgh and Westminster. Questions whether provisions
of a Bill are within the competence of the Scottish
Parliament may be determined by the Privy Council upon
a reference under s 33. Issues which thereafter may arise are
encapsulated in the definition of 'devolution issue' in cl 1,
Pt I of Sched 6 of the *Scotland Act*. The evident purpose of
the 'fast-track' procedure specified in Sched 6 is that these
matters will be determined by the Judicial Committee of the
Privy Council,[155] not the House of Lords. Provision also is
made for direct references to the Privy Council by the Law
Officers (ss 33–4).

The devolution structure thus does display several characteristics commonly found in the federal systems of
common law countries.

ABSENCE OF POWER AND INCONSISTENCY BETWEEN LAWS

There is a distinction to be made between questions arising
as to the limits *inter se* of the respective powers of two or
more legislatures, and the resolution of conflicts between
laws made in exercise of concurrent legislative power with
respect to the same subject-matter. Questions 'between
powers' are not the same as those 'between laws made
under powers'.[156] Section 28(7) of the *Scotland Act* empha-
sizes that the statute does not affect the power of the
Parliament of the United Kingdom to make laws for
Scotland. It may be that legislation with respect to the
'domestic affairs' of Scotland will not, as a political matter,
be enacted at Westminster against the wishes of Holyrood.
But the resourcefulness of litigants is such that points may
be taken that, whatever the best intentions of legislators at

---

[155] The composition of that body will not include those who have held high
judicial office in the Commonwealth: McFadden, 'The Scottish Parliament:
Provisions for Dispute Resolution' [1998] *Juridical Review* 221 at 233. The same
author makes the point (at 229) that a pre-assent ruling in favour of validity
appears to pre-empt a post-assent ruling in a dispute arising on actual facts.

[156] *O'Sullivan v Noarlunga Meat Ltd* [1957] AC 1 at 27. See also *R v Winneke; Ex
parte Gallagher* (1982) 152 CLR 211 at 216; *Flaherty v Girgis* (1987) 162 CLR 574 at
588.

Westminster may have been, they produced legislation with respect to a particular subject concurrently, and inconsistently, with laws made in Scotland.

No doubt laws of the United Kingdom have paramountcy. But by what criteria is the presence of inconsistency to be ascertained and adjudged? Are these criteria concerned solely with the adjustment of relations between legislatures or also concerned with the protection of citizens against being twice vexed with respect to the one matter? Does the repeal of, or operation of, a 'sunset clause' in a paramount law revive the operation of a pre-existing law of the subordinate legislature?[157] If that be so, 'inconsistent' is better understood as 'inoperative'.

Questions of inconsistency arise at a further level. The *Scotland Act* attributes paramountcy also to Community law and to 'the Convention rights', an expression which has the same meaning as given in the *Human Rights Act* 1998 (UK). This paramountcy is expressed in s 29(2)(d) in terms of the 'legislative competence' of the Scottish Parliament and 'so far as' any provision of legislation is 'outside' that competence, it 'is not law' (s 29(1)).

However, 'Community law' is defined in s 126(9) by reference to rights, powers, liabilities, obligations and restrictions 'from time to time created or arising by or under the Community Treaties' and by reference to remedies and procedures 'from time to time' provided by or under those Treaties. Accordingly, the content of Community law will fluctuate and with it the 'legislative competence' of the Scottish Parliament. The existence or lack of legislative power usually is adjudged at the time of enactment, and with final effect at that stage. A Scottish law, though, may be within legislative competence when enacted but, by reason of subsequent changes in Community law, may be rendered 'not law' to the extent of and whilst it is 'incompatible', that is to say 'inconsistent', with Community law. Indeed, the adoption in s 29(2)(d) of

[157] Section 109 of the Australian Constitution can produce this result: *Butler v Attorney-General (Vict)* (1961) 106 CLR 268.

the criterion of 'incompatibility' is indicative of inconsistency as disclosed in the decisions dealing with the impact from time to time of Community law upon primary or delegated legislation from Westminster.

What may be expected is the development of a body of authority, perhaps assisted by recourse to experience elsewhere over long periods, as to what is involved in this notion of 'incompatibility'. I have referred to some of the issues earlier in this lecture.[158]

In other respects, s 29 does deal with the relationship of the legislative powers *inter se* of those of the Scottish Parliament and the United Kingdom Parliament. It does so by denying power to the former, thereby confirming the exclusivity of the power of the latter, with respect to such things as 'reserved matters' (s 29(2)(b)). The phrase 'relates to reserved matters' receives further explanation in s 29(3) and (4).[159] Plainly, s 29 will present issues of characterization upon which there will turn the competency of the Scottish Parliament.

CHARACTERIZATION OF LAWS

Questions of classification or characterization are significant in the application of the principles of private international law. The 'classification' of a claim reveals the relevant rule for the choice of law. Characterization of written laws

---

[158] See text accompanying fnn 122–36.
[159] This states:

'(3) For the purposes of this section, the question whether a provision of an Act of the Scottish Parliament relates to a reserved matter is to be determined, subject to subsection (4), by reference to the purpose of the provision, having regard (among other things) to its effect in all the circumstances.

'(4) A provision which—

(a) would otherwise not relate to reserved matters, but

(b) makes modifications of Scots private law, or Scots criminal law, as it applies to reserved matters,

is to be treated as relating to reserved matters unless the purpose of the provision is to make the law in question apply consistently to reserved matters and otherwise.'

arises at a different level in the domestic legal order where (*a*) legislative competence is denied if certain criteria apply, or (*b*) such competence is conferred only if certain criteria are satisfied. Section 29 is an example of category (*a*).

The constitutional scheme in the United States and Australia is to allot to the central authority legislative powers with respect to specified subjects and the residue to the States. The doctrine established by Marshall CJ, as indicated earlier in this lecture, is to give to the terms of the specific grants their full effect before ascertaining the residue.[160] In Canada, the allotment by s 91 of the *British North America Act* 1867 (Imp) of specific powers to the federal legislature was accompanied by the enumeration in s 92 of a list of powers conferred exclusively upon the Provinces, with the residue reserved by s 91 to the federal legislature. The result of these differing arrangements has been contrasting and fluctuating methods of interpretation, with a general perception that in significant respects the Provinces are in a stronger position in Canada than are the States in the United States and in Australia.[161]

The *Scotland Act* follows neither model. The designation of subject-matter is confined to that in respect of which the subordinate legislature, the Scottish Parliament, is denied legislative competence.

The arrangement may have a closer affinity to that considered, with respect to Northern Ireland, by Lord Atkin in *Gallagher v Lynn*.[162] There was excepted from the generally expressed power of Stormont the making of laws 'in respect of ... [t]rade with any place out of [Northern Ireland]'.[163] The issue was not whether the law in question, which licensed the production and distribution of milk, fell within any exclusive head of power of the subordinate

---

[160] See Mason, 'The Role of a Constitutional Court in a Federation: A Comparison of the Australian and the United States Experience' (1986–7) 16 *Federal Law Review* 1 at 4–8, 13–21.

[161] Field, 'The Differing Federalisms of Canada and the United States' (Winter 1992) 55 *Law and Contemporary Problems* 107; Zines, 'Judicial Review in Australia and Canada' in Hodgins *et al.* (eds), *Federalism in Canada and Australia: Historical Perspectives, 1920–1988*, (1989) at 104–29.   [162] [1937] AC 863.

[163] *Government of Ireland Act* 1920 (Imp), s 4(7).

legislature, as might have been the case in Canada. It was whether it fell outside the competence of Stormont and thus solely within the general powers of Westminster. Nevertheless, Lord Atkin applied the expression 'pith and substance', drawn from decisions construing the Canadian Constitution,[164] to conclude, with unhappy resonances in patent law,[165] that the law was not passed 'in respect of' trade with any place outside Northern Ireland. This was because its 'true nature and character' or 'pith and substance' was the protection of the health of the inhabitants of the Province. This was so notwithstanding the law might 'incidentally affect trade with County Donegal' where the appellant produced milk for sale in Londonderry.[166] The 'pith and substance' criterion has, with force, been criticized as inapplicable in its translation from Canada to Northern Ireland, given the differences in the respective constitutional frameworks.[167]

If the Parliament at Stormont had had a specific grant with respect to trade extending beyond that Province, but none with respect to public health within the Province, would it have been an answer by the appellant that the law under which he had been convicted was a law with respect to public health as well as a law with respect to his trade from County Donegal? This is a fanciful illustration to make the point that a law may display various characteristics.

If the question be whether the law is supported by a designated head of power, validity is not denied by the circumstance that the law displays other characteristics.[168] That proposition requires qualification where the characteristic is specified as a denial of what otherwise would be within power. At least where the denial of legislative

---

[164] See *Belfast Corporation v O D Cars Ltd* [1960] AC 490 at 520.

[165] *Clark v Adie* (1877) 2 App Cas 315 at 320; *C Van Der Lely NV v Bamfords Limited* [1963] RPC 61 at 75; *Catnic Components Limited v Hill & Smith Limited* [1982] RPC 183 at 242–3.   [166] [1937] AC 863 at 870.

[167] Hadfield, *The Constitution of Northern Ireland* (1989) at 85–7.

[168] *Murphyores Incorporated Pty Ltd v The Commonwealth* (1967) 136 CLR 1; *Actors and Announcers Equity Association v Fontana Films Pty Ltd* (1982) 150 CLR 169 at 191–2; *Leask v The Commonwealth* (1996) 187 CLR 579 at 621–2, 633.

competence amounts to a guarantee of individual rights and freedoms, it should be given a liberal construction[169].

TERRITORIAL CONNECTION

There is excepted from the legislative competence of the Scottish Parliament provisions which 'would form part of the law of a country or territory other than Scotland' (s 29(2)(a)).

In *Union Steamship Co of Australia Pty Ltd v King*,[170] the High Court held that the fact that a ship engaged in inter-state trade and commerce was registered in New South Wales was sufficient connection with that State to enable its legislature to apply its laws to that ship and to justify the application to seamen employed upon it of a State statute entitling them as against their employer to workers' compensation benefits. Even a remote and general connection between the circumstances on which a law operated and the State enacting it would suffice to confer validity. In Canada, the extraterritorial competence of the Provinces is seen rather differently. The Supreme Court of Canada has held that Manitoba could not create a statutory right of action for damages against out-of-Province firms which introduce pollutants into rivers flowing eventually into Manitoba and thereby destroying Manitoba fisheries.[171] The doctrine was explained in *Churchill Falls (Labrador) Corporation Limited v The Attorney-General of Newfoundland*:

> Where the pith and substance of the provincial enactment is in relation to matters which fall within the field of provincial legislative competence, incidental or consequential effects on extra-provincial rights will not render the enactment *ultra vires*. Where, however, the pith and substance of the provincial enactment is the derogation from or elimination of extra-provincial

169 *Clunies-Ross v The Commonwealth* (1984) 155 CLR 193 at 201–2.
170 (1988) 166 CLR 1.
171 *Interprovincial Co-Operatives Limited v Manitoba* [1976] 1 SCR 477.

rights then, even if it is cloaked in the proper
constitutional form, it will be *ultra vires*.[172]

In neither federation is the competence of State or
Provincial legislation made to turn upon the question
whether it would form part of a law of a country or territory other than that of the enacting legislature. Whether the
measure did form part of the law of another polity would
depend upon its recognition as effective by the law of that
polity. The law might, under the rules of private international law there obtaining, be picked up as the *lex causae* in
particular actions tried in the courts of that polity. Full faith
and credit might be required under federal legislation or by
reason of an imperative requirement found in the text or
structure of the constitution.[173]

These are some of the issues which may lie ahead. They
may require the exercise by counsel of more than those
skills of statutory construction which they have applied
hitherto to legislation emanating from Westminster.

DICEY, EUROPE, AND SCOTLAND

To an observer versed in the ways of federalism, it has
appeared a little strange that, for a quarter of a century,
those British lawyers who seek to come to grips with the
doctrinal significance of membership of what is now the
European Union have tended to assert that European law
and institutions are separate and distinct from the system at
the head of which stands the Parliament at Westminster.
The subject fundamentally involves questions of constitutionalism, although that has not been a preferred term.
When the term 'federalism' has been used, it often has been
employed pejoratively, to suggest centralization of power

---

[172] [1984] 1 SCR 297 at 332.

[173] See the trilogy of decisions in the Supreme Court of Canada: *De Savoye v
Morguard Investments Ltd* [1990] 3 SCR 1077 at 1100–1; *Hunt v T & N Plc* [1993] 4
SCR 289; *Tolofson v Jensen* [1994] 3 SCR 1022 at 1063–4; the discussion thereof by
Professor Castel in ch 2 of his *Canadian Conflict of Laws*, 4th edn (1997); and the
judgment of Gaudron J in *The Commonwealth v Mewett* (1997) 191 CLR 471 at 524–5.

rather than its more accurate meaning of the division of power.

My conclusion is that use of the 1972 Act to reconcile the new legal order with the teachings of Dicey is unsatisfying. There must be force in the observation that the existence at Westminster of mechanisms for divorcing the United Kingdom from Europe does not deny the present reality of the constitutional arrangements between them.[174] That reality is that Westminster does not enjoy legislative omni-competence. Its retained competence is inherent, rather than derived or delegated from the European Union. In contrast, that of the Scottish legislature is derived from Westminster and is not inherent.

[174] Harden, 'The Constitution of the European Union' [1994] *Public Law* 609 at 612. See also Birkinshaw, 'European Integration and United Kingdom Constitutional Law' (1997) 3 *European Public Law* 57 at 86–90.

Index